ALSO BY MALTI BHOJWANI

Thankfulness Appreciation Gratitude – My Journal

Don't Think of a Blue Ball

Buat Apa Susah – Rahasia Menciptakan Kehidupan Impian (Bahasa Indonesia)

The Mind Spa – Ignite Your Inner Life Coach

In honour of my ancestors and parents

Bhojwani - Aswani bradri

Melwani - Vaswani bradri

my father
Lachmandas Naraindas Bhojwani 1939-2020

my mother
Maya Bhojwani

MASTERING
YOUR
LIFE

Malti Bhojwani

First paperback edition March 2021

Edited by Rich Andrew

Book design by @sdkstories

Audiobook read by Jenn Henry

Excerpts reprinted by permission

ISBN 978-1-09837-182-1(paperback)

ISBN 978-1-09837-183-8 (eBook)

www.maltibhojwani.com

CONTENTS

LIVING WITH JOY

This book came about when I realised the last ten years of my life have been a manifestation of all my dreams. When I published my earlier books, I had just begun to subscribe to the paradigm of creating a joyful life rather than just trying to get my survival needs met = to not die. In the last decade, I took the leap of faith, allowing life to unfold without control and fear. I started to believe, and now that I am genuinely living it, my past books have become "old", as will this one as soon as it goes to publication - the author's plight.

It was in its final stages of formatting when I had just come out of serving mandatory hotel quarantine. Surprisingly, I enjoyed the time to myself, even though I always assumed I was an extrovert. It demonstrated to me how much I had grown to love myself and my company.

I had always wanted to use the words "stop press", and I got my chance!

Soon after, I came out of quarantine and was happily chilling with family and friends in Sydney; a text message from my brother early one morning totally knocked me over. Our mother was taken by ambulance to the hospital – she had just had a major heart attack, entirely out of the blue.

I had never been more fragile and yet strong at the same time. I thought I had overcome my fear of losing a loved one, but I had not.

She seemed fine the day before but woke up with some unease, and the next thing she knew, the paramedics took her to the emergency room. She was sent for an angiogram where they tried to balloon and stent her artery, but her LAD left anterior descending artery was too blocked. After she underwent bypass surgery, we got to see her, all tubed up in the Intensive Care Unit, ICU.

My mum's biggest fear was to "fall sick". "Open-heart surgery" was something she regarded as the most painful thing a person could endure, and here she was. We thought she was out of the woods when they extubated her, and she could talk to us. She shared her lucid "hallucinations" about my father, who had passed precisely 14 months earlier in the same hospital. She saw him pulling her blanket. She really believed that nurses were playing with loud laughing bags in the quiet ICU to cheer her up because they knew how very sad she was, "her heart was broken".

Were they the effects of the anaesthesia and strong pain medications, or maybe the thin veil between life and death, had become even more refined. Perhaps it was her choice to make, "shall I stay or shall I go"? My dad had similar experiences, hearing voices, seeing figures in front of his hospital bed too when he was about to "check out".

Two sleepless nights later, I woke up to a call from the hospital that Maya had gone into cardiac arrest in the early morning. Her heart had stopped.

However, it "just so happened" that a heart transplant surgeon was about to leave the hospital in an Uber that had just pulled up when he got the call. His team of surgeons and the technicians who operated the heart and lung machine called ECMO, (Extracorporeal membrane oxygenation) were also around at three a.m in the morning. Maya was revived and put on the machine.

We were called in to be updated on all the possible side effects and complications and to sign consent forms after the fact. That night, I felt like all the air had been sucked out of my lungs. I was not ready to lose her to the light. I could not fathom this planet without this wonderful lady who had been my mother for almost fifty years. I cried buckets and dragged myself to the hospital daily, silently reciting my mantras, praying and at the same time letting go.

I stopped needing her to love me, I just loved her and wanted her to have a pain-free life experience of joy and dignity, and if not, then I was ready to let go and wanted her to go to the light. I surrendered, knowing I had no regrets or words unsaid or deeds undone to her.

Three days later, she gained strength. I guess her Self and her Soul finally made the choice to stay. She was then successfully weaned off the machine. Yes, medical science saved her life, but she had been butchered. The emotional and physical healing was going to take some time. At first, she was so upset with us for "bringing her back", she did not believe that we had nothing to do with it. Her higher self and divine laws chose to stick around for "round 2". Slowly, she started to get better and better every day.

I stumbled on Emile Coue's work, namely his affirmation,

"Every day in every way, I am getting better and better", and I asked mum to recite it, and I prayed for her to believe it. She did. She got better and better every day. As I was the one "on-the-ground", I found myself typing detailed messages about her condition daily to send to family and friends. I got into the habit of referring to her by name, Maya.

It must have been about then when I started to see her as Maya - a woman who had her own desires and preferences. Her personality was unmasked from all the roles I had seen her play her entire life - mother, carer, wife. I think her attacks and imminent recovery gave her a renewed zest to live for herself for life's sake.

At the time of publication, she continues to get better and better every day. She is still with us.

In that time, my daughter and husband helped keep me sane and happy, and they topped it off when they surprised me with a fabulous month-long celebration for my fiftieth birthday. I am feeling energetic and enthusiastic these days. Like my mum, I, too, have been re-born, this time without the shackles of fear that weighed me down before.

The last fifty years were the preparation for the rest of my wonderful life, and I am so ready. Although I enjoyed the entire roller coaster ride and wouldn't change anything now, it is far easier to say this in hindsight. This book was born to share with you what I now know so that perhaps you can let go of fears and insecurities and begin to truly live your life joyfully.

CHAPTER 1:
EXPANDING THE OBSERVER YOU ARE

Welcome — to the first day of the rest of your life.

Awesome! I am so happy that you have chosen to embark on this journey of self-discovery and self-mastery with me. It takes immense courage and humility to pause, stop in our tracks, and look around at what we have created. Accepting that we have indeed played a part in creating the outcomes in our relationships, our health, our lives takes a mindset of ownership - of mastery.

Many of us can go through our lives absolutely ignorant, running our lives on autopilot. It takes a deliberate choice to look within and become new architects and authors designing what we want the rest of our lives to look and feel like. This moment is the start of changing the trajectory of your life.

I want to acknowledge you for coming this far. Indeed, many of the things you have done have worked, or you wouldn't be here, but there comes a time when we start to realise that what got us here may not take us to where we want to go. Many of us may have also realised that we no longer feel the same connection with the people in our lives as we used to; we can no longer relate to or resonate with each other. Though this may feel sad in some ways, know that it is simply a sign of your own evolution. There comes a point where things don't feel as fulfilling — even the achievement of some goals don't feel as wonderful as we thought they might — when we start to search for more meaning in our lives.

I was born in Singapore, my dad, Lachman, migrated here after the India/Pakistan partition from India when he was fourteen, and my mom, Maya, moved from China when she was five. When I was growing up, I was pretty privileged. We had everything that we wanted, but I suffered from extremely low self-esteem and self-worth as I stepped into my early teens.

I was an obese child, teased and bullied in school. Then, my dad lost money, packed us up, and moved us to Australia. At a very young age, I already started to feel like a victim, that life would serve me these events and circumstances, and all I could do was react to them.

When I was twenty-six, I found myself overweight, penniless and divorced with a six-year-old daughter. I didn't have much of a career or work prospects, felt incredibly alone, my self-esteem depleted. I looked outside of myself for appreciation, for acknowledgements of acceptance just to make me feel good about myself. Still, the thing is that when you're reliant on the outside world and others to make you feel worthy or good enough, then you will never ever feel good enough. You'll always be waiting for that next point of recognition, for that next person to like you, want you, compliment you.

"The funny thing is that the caterpillar never realised that she was always already indeed a butterfly inside."

I love the symbolism of a butterfly for transformation because I've never heard of the butterfly that went back to being a caterpillar. In fact, the caterpillar was always a butterfly inside; it kept going with its gut to initiate each step it took, unaware of what its future held. Then, just when it almost gave up, it grew beautiful, mighty wings, broke out of the chrysalis and soared high up, seeing the same world from a new, higher vantage point. (Interesting fact: Recent research found that caterpillars indeed initiate their wriggle from their guts)

Transforming from being a victim reacting to life to mastering your life is all about choice. It starts from a basic expanded assumption that you are indeed creating in every single moment. We are making assumptions all the time anyway, so why not choose the ones that will help you get to where you say you so want to get?

Let's look at assumptions as beliefs. I used to live in the paradigm that life happened to me, but now I choose to see that everything I experience has a higher purpose, a meaning, a lesson. I can't prove this to you using science or logic, but no paradigm can be established or disproved. It just takes enough people to believe, and it becomes the "normal" way of thinking. Normal. What is normal, anyway? Would you prefer to be normal or to be happy?

"You never change things by fighting the existing reality.
To change something, build a new model that
makes the existing model obsolete."
- Buckminster Fuller

Mastery is not a destination we get to but rather a path. Mastery requires the humility to know that you never really "get" there, but you stay on course. The switch for me shifted from being a victim of other people and life circumstances to becoming a master of my own choices and life. It takes courage, immense courage, to make choices that are not aligned or not in line with societal norms, with what is considered normal. But I felt internally guided, and I was able to take that leap of faith, the path of the "so-called" deviant, even when I could not see what the road ahead was going to look like.

I chose adventure and freedom over stability and security. And I had many challenges and failures, failed relationships that broke my heart, rejections from job interviews, potential clients, editors and publishers that hurt my confidence. Countless business ventures that didn't work out, getting caught in scams that shattered my trust in my ability to make sound decisions.

I woke up many mornings on tear-drenched pillowcases, still gripping onto a phone that didn't ring—one failure and heartache after another. I felt deep anguish, desperation and hopelessness. But because somewhere inside, I knew that I was creating even the seeming losses around me, I knew that I could choose to create a different reality. I had just started to believe that I was worthy of greatness and that the "show wasn't over yet". This inner knowledge gave me the strength to get back up each time and continue to pursue happiness.

I took the lessons from the previous failures and tried again and again. And guess what? Failed again. Often, I would go back to feeling small, feeling like I am not worthy. I am not good enough. This is never going to work. Who do I think I am that I'm going to break out of this cycle? How can little fat me even try to create a life that I desire? Who do I think I am? But I found the wisdom to stop the incessant broken record of limiting thoughts, and I realised that I get to choose the next "playlist". I consciously chose to believe that I am worthy by virtue of the fact that I am alive. We were not put on this planet to suffer, and we were not put on this planet to feel undeserving of joy.

When we were born — in fact, at the moment of our conception — we received all the sustenance we needed through our mother's wombs. And we didn't have to earn it. We didn't have to work for it. It was ours, our birthright. But you need to wake up to it and own it. No amount of achievement, no new relationship, promotion or degree, no other level of success or dollars in the bank will make you feel worthy; only you can choose to embrace this truth and step into your worthiness. Only you can decide that you are worthy because you are alive. We are entitled to miracles.

The map is not the territory, but a map is still an excellent way to understand the terrain.

We view the world, our options, and ourselves through filters, and what's not helpful about it is most of us don't even know that we are looking through these filters. Beliefs are these filters. We inherited some beliefs about ourselves and how to navigate life in utero and formed some of them when we were really young, even before we had the proper vocabulary to describe them. Some of them worked for us up to a certain point, but then, if we genuinely want to transform our lives, we need to be able to see clearly what beliefs have been running us up to now and how can we break them, let light shine through them, and reframe the ones that have passed their "use-by" date. We need to reassess their validity.

Epigenetics' study explains how our beliefs and ingrained strategies to cope with life's stresses may have been "pre-programmed" and inherited through our DNA. Traditional genetics describes how the DNA sequences in our genes passed from one generation to the next; epigenetics describes the passing down of the way genes are used - through chemical tags attached to our DNA.

So essentially, we have inherited the beliefs that supported our ancestors' survival in their times, even though the world we now live in does not have the same challenges for most of us. What got us here may not take us to where we want to go. Let me share an example from my ancestry.

I have heard stories of how my maternal grandfather climbed the steep rope ladder on the side of a ship as it left the Indian shores in the possibility of finding "greener pastures". He docked in China and managed to amass great wealth. Similarly, my paternal family fled India to settle in Singapore and struggled in the early days to make a living. As you can see, my ancestors inadvertently may have passed down courage on the one hand but also the mindset of lack. They lived in a "trance of scarcity", with a philosophy that "there is never enough". It's no surprise that they lived their lives in fierce competition, mistrust, saving and hoarding.

In a way, their inherited belief systems allowed them to survive, propagate, and us to be born in the first place; it got us here - alive now. The irony is that they worked hard so that we wouldn't have to face their plight. When will you decide to reject the "life-sentences" of our forefathers, "to suffer", and "just survive" and instead subscribe to the wisdom that you can let it go and thrive in this lifetime?

Formed, pre-birth and in our childhood, many of us go through our lives reinforcing our beliefs. That's what people call a self-fulfilling prophecy. An example of that would be when I had a belief that "life is hard" or that "money is the root of evil," then how do you think my life experience panned out? How open was I to attracting wealth? If I had a belief that "you just can't trust people," then my first instinct would be to mistrust anyone who came into my life. The need to be right about my beliefs would attract circumstances that confirmed them.

In the following chapters, we are going to look at our beliefs much more closely. Are they serving us, helping us, or not? Can we see through the veil and make new choices? Can we reframe them even if we can't pinpoint them specifically?

We're going to look deeply at human needs based on the old work of Abraham Maslow. We'll look at our values and priorities through the lens of the levels of consciousness. Have you noticed that your priorities have changed? What used to be so important to you, maybe just a while ago, really has no space in your life right now. And that's not a bad thing. But we just need to know and be aware that they have shifted. What are your priorities now?

"We see the world not as it is but as we are."
- Anaïs Nin

The Observer – Action = Results "OAR" model - Newfield Coaching

Transformation can occur when we "shift our viewpoint and change the observer that we are in such a way that it is possible to develop a new set of actions." In his publication, "From Knowledge to Wisdom - Essays on the

Crisis in Contemporary Learning, Julio Olalla, founder of the Newfield Network, uses distinctions to help us understand the observer we are.

When I was in this victim mindset, I saw the world as hard, punishing. I felt that when anything went wrong, it had to be someone's fault, and if I could not find anyone to blame, then I blamed myself. I saw that people couldn't be trusted. I constantly reacted to life situations and people's behaviours in my life without ever pausing to evaluate the part I played in the circumstances I found myself in. All my conversations with my loved ones would start with, "do you know what happened to me?" My life was just a series of reacting to all the happenings from the outside. I had grievances about almost everything and everyone around me. I formed a habit of complaining and frowning. But when I shifted the observer that I was from victimhood to mastery, I started to see perceived "obstacles" through the lens of acceptance and gratitude, and I chose to learn, grow, and trust that I had it in me to at least take the next step. That paradigm shift completely transformed my life. I was able to see new radical options for action as they opened up for me when I was no longer limited by my old paradigm of seeing myself as a victim.

How many times in your life have you tried to take action to change your behaviour? You do this hoping that you will arrive at a completely different place but find yourself still stuck in patterns of doing very similar things? Maybe slightly different but definitely not enough to take you to a new place? Well, that's because how you perceive yourself and your various options in life — is so dependent on your level of self-awareness and consciousness.

In this chapter, we want to deepen your understanding of yourself to widen the aperture so that you have new options for action available to you. In the later chapters, we will look at what those actions could be. When we start thinking about wanting to change our lives' outcomes, wanting to transform our lives, we often only think about changing our actions. What can I do differently? What should I start doing or stop doing or do more of? We think that actions will lead to the outcomes or the results. That is true, but to truly explore new actions, we must first expand the way we perceive.

> *"The mind, once stretched by a new idea, never returns to*
> *its original dimensions."*
> *- Ralph Waldo Emerson*

In the OAR model, O stands for the observer, A for action, and R for results.

EXPANDING THE APERTURE

The observer is like an aperture in a camera; the size and the depth will determine what you see externally and what you know about yourself internally. It's through that lens that you can make decisions and take action. Then, from your action, you will create outcomes and results in your life. Expanding the observer that we are will deepen our self-awareness and connect us with pure consciousness.

"The key to growth is the introduction of higher dimension
of consciousness into our awareness."
- Lao Tzu

Consciousness refers to our level of self-awareness. Higher consciousness is the consciousness of a higher self, a God-self, or the part of the human mind capable of transcending animal instincts. When we deepen our self-awareness and raise our consciousness, we connect with the essence of ourselves that realises that we are, in fact, pure consciousness. The source of all creation is "pure consciousness," "pure potentiality". Life is an expression of this - from unmanifest (soul) into the manifest (body and ego). We are spiritual beings having a human experience.

"We are not human beings having a spiritual experience;
we are spiritual beings having a human experience."
- Pierre Teilhard de Chardin

That veil lifts when we realise that as a spirit being human, streams of infinite love, joy, and abundance have always been our birthright, but our fears and beliefs are what block its flow to us.

The critical practice that made the most significant difference in my life was to instil the diligent practice of meditation. Meditation is the most powerful way to connect with my true essence — with pure consciousness. And I found that when I started to meditate regularly, I attracted opportunities into my life. Life became synchronous. You know, those seeming coincidences, those miracles we talk about, the magic. I'm sure you've experienced it too, those inexplicable times when things just worked out.

If I had an extra dollar for every instance, I met someone "by chance", from an Uber driver to a cashier who had a message to show me that I was being guided.

When you notice these synchronicities, know that you are flowing with cosmic energy, but you can't have control and flow at the same time. Trusting means letting go of control. Think of a child gripping onto the handrails on a slide, only causing friction. Try letting go and doing a big figurative or vocal "wheeeeeee!" instead. It just makes life so much more fun and your soul's job that much easier.

Haven't you had times in your life when you had no clue how — you could not have orchestrated it yourself using your logical mind — but things just fell into place? You are at the right place, right time; the person who you were thinking of called, causing you to show up somewhere at the perfect time, and then the same opportunity that you've been waiting for all your life shows up for you. As you deepen your awareness and raise your consciousness, these seeming coincidences will become frequent. Synchronicities will happen, and you will be there to notice and then grab those opportunities and walk down those paths because they will feel so right for you.

"The body is anchored in the here and
now while the mind travels to the past and future."
- The Buddha

CENTRING – A MICRO-MEDITATION

Centring helps us gain awareness of our state, our physical body, our emotions, and our thoughts.

When our eyes are open, all our senses are outward. When we close our eyes, we bring our attention inward. Let's do this together now. Close your eyes. Now with your eyes closed, notice and become aware of your body. Notice if you have any tension or strain around your forehead, cheeks, neck, shoulders, arms, and feet. And then consciously just let it go. Relax.

Now bring your awareness to your breath. Take a deep, conscious breath and feel it expanding in your body. Visualise your breath in your physical body and imagine that it's in the centre of your body. Halfway between front and back, halfway between left and right, and halfway between the top of your head and the soles of your feet. As you continue to breathe into the centre of your body, notice your emotions.

What are you feeling right now? Tell yourself it's okay to feel this way. Whatever you're feeling is perfect. And then listen to the sounds around you, perhaps the humming of an air conditioner or fan in your surroundings and listen a layer deeper; listen to the silence. There is always silence beneath the sounds. There is always calm beneath the chaos. Pause to be quiet for a few moments while you experience this feeling of being centred.

Silence is the centre of language. Acceptance is the centre of emotion. And you're breathing into the centre of your body. Now, gently open your eyes and notice how you feel and try to keep this feeling of centredness with you as much as you can. We can't stay centred all day. But what we can do is be aware of when we're off-centre and bring ourselves back.

After this chapter, my invitation to you is this: make it a point to find moments in your day to centre. It doesn't need to take long at all. Just find a comfortable position. You can even centre when you're standing up with your eyes open. We go through our lives with our eyes open; we're interacting with our eyes open. And often when we feel off-centre, it's just great to be able to come back to centre. Just connect. Breathe into your belly. Notice your feelings. Accept them. Then find the silence. And here you are. We often forget how related our body, minds, and emotions are.

Think of centring as a micro meditation helping to align body, emotion, and thought. In the later chapters, we're going to explore a more profound method of meditation.

REFLECTION

Are you the same observer that you were when you were younger? What new assumptions have you made about yourself and the world as you started growing up? Are any of these assumptions still valid? Take a couple of moments to ponder these questions.

The fundamental goal of noticing the observer you are is to offer you the opportunity to shift your perspective. Can you start looking at some of the situations that you saw as problems differently? Can you now start looking at them as opportunities? Can you look at your past failures as feedback? Can you look at things that seem impossible from the point of view of "what if"? What outdated beliefs are you ready to let go of?

Would you rather be right about your default way of thinking, staying dissatisfied, and continue to experience more of the same? Or are you willing to consider another point of view and see things from a different way even if it feels uncomfortable or abnormal? Well, it's your choice. It has become a "common" belief that life is hard, and hence subscribing to a belief that we can actually enjoy life and expect positive outcomes is like not facing reality. Instead, isn't it time you challenge what is stopping you from subscribing to believe that simply having fun and pursuing joy is why we exist?

I have put together exercises, videos, and other resources that you can use along with this book in the downloadable workbook or visit https://maltibhojwani.com/myl.html

CHAPTER 2:

CONNECTING WITH PURPOSE THROUGH JOY

When you can be all that you need to be, be your higher, most evolved self, then you can do the actions that will bring you what you say you so want. When your very being radiates your soul's purpose, then the actions you take will be inspired by your purpose. That's what is called purposeful living. Many of us had the belief that if we only "had" what we wanted, then we would "do" what is needed to "be" happy, but in truth, it's the other way around: "be-do-have." When we are (be) happy first, we will be inspired to "do," and the "have" will follow naturally!

"Musicians must make music, artists must paint, poets must
write if they are ultimately to be at peace with themselves.
What humans can be, they must be."
- Abraham Maslow

PURPOSE

Do you know what you are on this planet to do? Why do you exist? What is uniquely yours? Having a clear sense of purpose can be a guiding light.

It can act as an internal compass to support us and help us, especially when we have to make decisions and choices in our lives. So what is your purpose? Have you thought about it before? Many of us have an apparent purpose in our minds; many of us have written it down somewhere. But for many of us, it's a sense that we have within us that we haven't really articulated yet.

So today, we're going to craft a two-word purpose statement. It's called the core process and was taught to me by Andrew Chua, my friend, and developed in the '70s by Chris Bowles and Janet Mills.

I love this process because it requires us to connect with moments of joy and fulfilment in our lives and then associate those moments with words to create a simple yet powerful two-word purpose statement. The most fundamental shift we can make in ourselves as the observer is to see that life is to be enjoyed and not merely endured.

Let's begin. In a while, I will direct you to a link that will help you craft your own two-word purpose. But for now, all you need to do is go back in time and reconnect with three of your happiest and most fulfilling moments, radiating who you are. I know you have many, but we only need to find three. And to get you started, let me share three of mine.

The first one that I'd love to share with you was relatively recent for me. I got remarried in 2019. When we were planning this wedding, both my husband and I had a fantastic time carefully planning the experience we wanted to create.

We wanted it to be intimate, so we chose who we wanted there explicitly to celebrate this joyful occasion with us. Although some close loved ones could not make it, like my younger brother Vishaal, sadly. We selected everything meticulously, from the venue to the decor, flowers, music and the menus. My talented daughter, Drishti, helped organise the dances and choreographies of all our favourite songs. She put on an incredible show and danced her heart out for us that night. My brother Sanjay gave a speech that captured my whole transformation in five minutes. Tears of self - acknowledgement and from feeling seen by my "big brother" flowed like a river, almost ruining my makeup. I realised then that a part of me had longed to be seen for who I'd always aspired to become.

The wedding was in Bali. And while we were planning it, my father, who was living in Australia at the time, was very sick. He had renal failure and had been on dialysis for quite some time. When I asked him if he would come up to the wedding, he never said yes. But neither did he say no. My dad was very reliable, and he never made promises that he wasn't sure he could keep. Mum promised to be there even though she didn't really know how she would swing it. Coming closer to the wedding, he said, well, I think I can make it. So he did dialysis on Friday morning, and they caught a plane from Sydney to Bali that night just in time to attend the wedding on Saturday.

All of us spent the entire weekend in a villa on the cliffs together with my then fiance's family. My parents were in their element – it was a respite filled with joy and beauty, from mum's life as dad's carer and dad as a patient living out his last months.

Immediately after the ceremony, my daughter surprised us. My dad was an excellent ballroom dancer; he loved cha-cha, jive, and rock n roll. And ten years before this date, my dad and I had performed the song Sway at a cousin's wedding. We had not rehearsed this dance for ten years. But my daughter called my dad and me to the dance floor. And my dad literally swayed me around the dance floor "like a flower bending in the breeze," That was the icing on the cake of my beautiful wedding. I got to experience what I like to call awesomeness, beauty in every way. Every sense of mine was fulfilled, and I felt utter joy.

My father passed away very soon after. But before that, while he was in his last days in the hospital, then a nursing home, he still watched the videos of that dance that we had together. And he showed them off to all the nurses and caretakers. My wedding was indeed one of my happiest moments.

The second one I'd like to share with you is what I'm doing right now. I love to share stories and models and help bring them to life through writing, coaching and facilitating workshops. I absolutely love it. When people tell me that they could change their way of seeing themselves and start living a much more joyful life, a less reactive life, that really makes me feel fulfilled. When someone tells me that they have stopped raising a hand against their children, or they have stopped being impulsive or reactive to the people they love, that brings me immense joy.

The third memory I'd love to share with you is when my daughter was a baby in my arms while I sat in a rocking chair. And we listened — well, I don't know if she was listening — but I would play the song A Groovy Kind of Love by Phil Collins. And there was one line: "Wouldn't you agree? Baby, you and me, we've got a groovy kind of love." And we do. Every time I think of that, I think of us. It gives me so much joy.

Now it's your turn — stop and think of three of your happiest memories, your most fulfilling moments. The only prerequisite is that you have to have been in it, not watching it, not a spectator of it, but really present in that moment where it brought you immense joy and fulfilment. In NLP – Neuro-Linguistic Programming, this is called "being associated" into the internal representation, the memory and feelings of the experience.

They could be from your close relationships, something you practice daily, a one-off adventure or from your work and professional life. Perhaps a moment when you were coaching someone, mentoring someone; it could be a moment when the team was celebrating success. It could be anything; it just has to be personal and genuinely joyful to you. When you have thought of your three happiest moments, write them down with a keyword that will trigger your memory of them. For example, in my case, I wrote down "My Wedding," "Workshops/ Coaching," and "Groovy Kinda Love."

It's a straightforward process, and you're going to end up with two specific words—one verb and one noun that will act as an anchor to pure joy.

The first step is to find three continuous verbs, verbs that end in "ing". Here are some to choose from initiating, inspiring, empowering, enabling, igniting, unleashing, nurturing, nourishing, imagining, embracing, savouring, beholding, illuminating, releasing, attaining, honouring, welcoming, relating, loving, reaching, achieving, doing, organising, orchestrating, transforming, changing, supporting, facilitating, helping, finding, seeking, discovering, championing. Give yourself a few minutes. If you like, visit the resource link and see the list to look for some verbs that you feel resonate with all three of your happiest, most joyful and fulfilling moments.

The next step is to find three nouns. Here are some to choose from: communities, lives, families, people, hope, joy, love, faith, dreams, challenges, mountain, successes, significance, meaning, purpose, simplicity, destiny, light, knowledge, wisdom, adventure, excitement, generosity, abundance, fulfilment, worth, wonder, awesomeness, harmony, relationships, connections. Find three nouns that resonate across the three stories that you just reconnected with.

For me, verbs that stood out were orchestrating, igniting, unleashing, and the nouns were beauty, awesomeness, wonder. Once you've picked your three words, it's time to narrow them down to one verb and one noun. Take a few moments to do this by yourself, and then put them together and ensure that they make sense. They don't have to have meaning to anyone else; it only has to have meaning for you.

"People take different roads seeking fulfilment and happiness.
Just because they're not on your road doesn't mean they've gotten lost."
- Dalai Lama

Remember that these two words will act as a powerful switch to reconnect you with three of the most joyful moments in your life. I have had the privilege to behold awesomeness while I facilitated this very same two-word purpose process with my clients. And here are examples of some of the two-word purposes that they came up with: "cherishing connections," "exploring peace," "nurturing potential," "creating possibilities," "championing success," "mapping journeys," "connecting worlds," "transforming lives," "unlocking truth," and "unleashing possibilities."

If you're wondering what my two words are, they are "beholding awesomeness." The process took a while for me, like coffee — it took some time to brew. I was dabbling with "inspiring beauty," "creating beauty," or "transforming lives." My friend Andrew offered the word "behold," which was just the word I was searching for. In all my stories, I feel that I was there, sometimes creating it, sometimes inspiring it, sometimes orchestrating it, but for sure, being able to behold it, experience the awesomeness. Beholding brings to mind an image of holding both my hands cupped and accepting what is — it's the opposite of gripping or clenching onto what is transient, including life itself. I have found that it was the perfect balance of wanting and surrendering with all my manifested dreams and realised goals. The verb "beholding" resonated fully with me.

Often, you'll find yourself going through life, forgetting your two-word purpose. But then you'll come to a moment where you have to make a choice, especially a difficult one, between two equally good or equally challenging options. But then you will tune in to your two words and check in with yourself. So I check in with myself. If I say yes to this, will I be beholding awesomeness? Suppose I choose this path; could it lead to awesomeness? Checking in with your two words will help you make choices from your heart on a soul level, and we call that making purposeful choices, taking purposeful action.

Imagine what life would be if everything you did was aligned with your purpose. Purpose energy is like an Eveready battery. It does not run out; you never get tired or exhausted when you're living your purpose. It's very different from goal energy. Goal energy, yes, is sometimes fulfilling. You feel great when you achieve your goals, but it can also be draining because the goal is usually outside of you. And it's something that you move towards. And if you're like me, you often get to a destination, and what do you do? Well, if you said celebrate, then congratulations. That's awesome. Many times we don't even stop to celebrate; instead, we just set the next goal. But when you start living from purpose and setting goals aligned with your purpose, energy radiates from within. You can feel it tingling in your fingertips, in your feet, and it drives you, and you know what life to live. If you live your purpose daily and know that your purpose is connected to what brings you joy, meaning, and fulfilment, wouldn't that be awesome?

Now that you've picked your two words, write them on some post-it notes and stick them up all over your house, on your computer screen, by your bedside, your bathroom mirror so that you can look at them every day. You may find that it will grow on you, or like for me, it may brew like coffee, it might get stronger, or you might find that you want to tweak those words and change one of them.

Every time you're about to make a choice, check in. Do a quick centring. Now hold these two words within you. Imagine that your purpose is a flame or light bulb that's deep within you, and imagine that you can dial it up really bright. It's so radiant when you're living your purpose because you will be living the path that gives you fulfilment. When you follow that path, you, the Universe, will provide you with little gifts to line the course for you, letting you know you are in alignment with your soul. Fulfilment is different from immediate pleasures and happiness at the moment. Fulfilment is long term, and you feel satiated, as the word implies. When you can turn up that dial, the volume, the brightness, you will feel that lasting fulfilment within you.

"You can change the course of your life with your words."
- Anonymous

Even if these two words don't feel like they're powerful enough yet or don't capture your real life's purpose yet, trust me — follow the guiding light of these words, and your path will unfold. As you travel it, you will evolve, and then more and more, the next step will become visible. It's just like a GPS. Only when you start moving can the GPS guide you where next to go. But if you're stationary, it can't tell you anything. So think of lighting up your two-word purpose as igniting at least a little bit of the road ahead. Live your two-word purpose, enjoy it, live your purpose - fully.

"Great minds have purposes; others have wishes."
- Washington Irving

As we go through the next exercise, keep your purpose alive and lit within you. You will find that the observer you are now illuminated with your radiant purpose will see a much broader and more fulfilling future. I know it sounds cliché, but today is truly the first day of the rest of your life.

"Life is never made unbearable by circumstances
but only by lack of meaning and purpose."
- Viktor Frankl

Before we meet again in the next chapter, craft your two-word purpose if you haven't done so already. You will find it in the workbook as well as on the resource link: https://maltibhojwani.com/myl. html

CHAPTER 3:
VISUALISING THE FUTURE, ACCEPTING THE NOW

What does the best you look like?

Living purposefully, having meaning in your life? Having the body image, health, and vitality that you desire? Having finances enough, so you don't have to worry, and a sense that your career is on the right path? Knowing that you have enough of a support system, a community of friends and family in which you feel a deep sense of belonging? Having a significant other, someone you love who loves you, who will accept you as you are someone you can love as they are? Knowing that you can have fun, leisure, and recreation in your life? Feeling comfortable and joyful as you look around your work environment and your living space?

What does your best life look like? To discover this, we're going to explore the wheel of life.

The wheel of life that I've created has twelve spokes. The first spoke is health, and this includes well-being and physical health.

When was the last time you had a check-up? The second spoke is your finances. Look, I know many of you want to be billionaires and want to have Ferraris. Well, that's great if that's what you want, but is that what you need to make you feel financially successful and truly fulfilled in life? Check-in with yourself; what is it now? Forget what "they" say or what the world says. Who are they anyway? Aren't you tired of the "theys"? What is right for you? What would you like to have in your life to help you feel like you're living your best life?

Then, we'll look at love, romance, and connection — having that person who accepts you for who you are, whom you take for who they are, and whom you can be completely authentic with and be yourself in their company.

Having career satisfaction or career progression, knowing what the path looks like, and knowing where you want to get to.

Having a sense that you are evolving spiritually. This is not about religion but about being connected with your inner spirit — with your soul. Knowing what that means for you. Many of us don't know what our spiritual evolution path will look like, but we can trust our inner, knowing that we will continue to feel guided along the way that is right for us.

Having a sense of belonging with your friends and family. Having excellent empowering, trusting relationships with your colleagues.

Having a healthy sense of self-esteem and self-mastery.

The other spokes of the wheel of life include the physical environment, fun and recreation, personal growth, self-development, learning. And then we have one more spoke, which is called "other." This is for an area that might be unique to you, and maybe I didn't think of it. A few examples could be community service, making a difference to others, and giving back to society.

What would your best life look like? If you were to give each of these areas a nine or ten on a scale of zero to ten (one being the least satisfying and ten the most fulfilling), what would that look like? That's where we want to get to in this process. Be conscious that you may become more acutely aware of the delta or distance between where you perceive you currently are and where you would love to be as you do this exercise. Don't despair, and please don't worry about the "what-ifs." Worrying is literally visualising your worst nightmares when what you could be doing instead is focusing your thoughts on visualising your most desirable outcomes. The polar opposite of worrying about someone or something is to bless it.

I won't go into all twelve spokes in detail, but I want to speak to a few of them.

The first one is around health and physical well-being. What does being healthy look like to you? Do you love your body? It's the only one you've got.

As a child and teenager, I struggled with obesity. I managed to lose some weight and became "just" overweight. I wasn't happy with how I looked, and I used to call myself a victim of my genetics and hormones. But then, I challenged my limiting beliefs around weight loss by reframing them with helpful and empowering beliefs and took the bull by its horns. I asked for help and found all the support I needed. Slowly but steadily, I achieved the body that I had always dreamed of.

Are you comfortable in your body right now? If you are, that's great. And don't let anyone tell you that you need to be another way. If you are genuinely already happy with your body and health, celebrate it and never criticise yourself when you look in the mirror. Love and accept yourself. If you like, do a health check and ensure that this body will continue to carry you through life and support you as you live your purpose and achieve your dreams.

WHEEL OF LIFE — RELATIONSHIPS

The other spoke I want to focus on is about relationships and significant others. When I was younger, I remember now that I used to demand love and attention from the people around me. If I knew then what I know now about human behaviour, values, and needs, I think my past relationships would have been very different. On the one hand, I would have attracted very different people into my life. I might have been more compassionate and taken ownership instead of blaming them for being different from my expectation of how they "should" be. I might have realised that what I perceived in others as unfavourable was actually my own outdated beliefs causing me to react in my old patterns, provoking those around me to do the same.

Well, I'm glad that I went through this journey because I'm delighted now. I'm very blessed to have found someone who is so much fun to be with, compassionate, accepting, takes me as I am, has no intention to change me, yet inspires me to grow, seeing me in a higher light than I see myself. I wish for all of you to also have that in your lives.

If you are already in a relationship or a marriage, then check in with yourself. Can you make this work? Can you connect with what this person's deepest needs and values are and simply love them as they are? Is it at all possible that you are, in fact, projecting your own stuff onto this person? Can the two of you heal, evolve, and grow together?

When we consciously choose to accelerate our evolution and begin to transform our lives, grow, and step out of the status quo and comfort zones, it can become uncomfortable for the people in our lives. They may not be interested in changing; they could be far more evolved than we assume. If you would like to keep them in your life, be careful not to judge them or impose your ideas on them.

If you're single and searching, live what gives you joy - enjoy your life, and trust that when you are least in need for it to complete you because you have already become more whole, the most fantastic soul will waltz into your life, and you will "fall" in effortlessly. To support your belief system around breaking any walls built to protect your heart, visualise someone you can love and accept as they are. Let go of any preconceived criteria that this person must have for you to let them into your world. Open your heart, open your mind, and allow people in. Then check in with your own sense of purpose and values to see if you and this person can complement each other.

WHEEL OF LIFE — FINANCES

The other area I'd like to talk about is finances. There was a time when I did not know how I was going to pay rent. I'd get one coaching client who would pay just enough for me to survive for a few days. I was literally living hand to mouth, just in time, just enough. I was unhappy, miserable, and desperate.

I took a leap of faith and moved from India back to Singapore with nothing, absolutely nothing. I had a coach, Mark Hemstedt, who passed away in 2019. I remember calling him up and saying, "Mark, I'm thinking of coming back to Singapore, but everyone's telling me not to. They are saying, 'Don't come. How can you come back to Singapore if you don't have a real job? If you don't own a place? Things are so expensive here. Do you know how expensive it is to buy a car?' And blah, blah, blah." So, I asked him, "What should

I do?" And he reminded me, "Malti, you're an Indian girl, right?" I was like, "Yeah! But what does that have to do with anything?" He went on, "I recall you mentioned that you received some jewellery in your first marriage?" Me: "Yeah — so?" Mark: "Okay, where is that jewellery?" Me: "In a safe." Mark: "Where?" Me: "In a bank." Mark: "Where?" Me: "In Singapore."

My dearest friend Priya lent me the money to buy a ticket — that is how "broke" I thought I was back then. I moved to Singapore, went to that bank, took that jewellery, walked into a pawn shop, and sold it. If you know anything about Indian culture, the "common" belief is that jewellery is meant to be kept to be passed on, so for me, the willingness to let go of that archaic belief was a massive step in completely shattering some of my filters. I rented a room with that money — yes, a small room in a house, but it was enough.

Then, I thought, "What do I do now?" And so, I focused on myself. I exercised, I meditated, I did yoga, I walked to the beach every day. I was joyful, grateful and happy. And then slowly, things just started to change. I was able to shift my mindset from scarcity to abundance, and that transformed my finances.

I was offered a job that had nothing to do with my passion and purpose, but I took it for the income. I didn't enjoy it but was grateful for the opportunity to learn and earn; but again, I just knew that I had to let go of it to truly give my dreams the wings to come true, so I quit even though I knew there were no more safety nets. There was no more gold in the bank, and I had to make it. And guess what? I did. But what it taught me that whole time was that I didn't need a lot to live on. In fact, I could thrive, be happy on very little. My elevated vibration of gratitude, appreciation and joy attracted surprising new opportunities into my life. For me now, everything more is extra is a bonus — and that's having a mindset of abundance. Abundance flowed into my life in such unexpected ways that I could not have conjured it up alone.

In the later chapters, we will explore practices that you can do to create new neural pathways and raise your consciousness out of the paradigm of fear and lack so that you, too, can attract abundance into your life.

For now, define for yourself very clearly what living your best life would look like on every one of the spokes and create a vision board based on that.

1. Health (physical, emotional well-being)

2. Finances

3. Love — significant other/romance

4. Career satisfaction/progression

5. Spiritual evolution (sense of self, meaning, & purpose)

6. Sense of belonging/friends & family

7. Relationships with colleagues

8. Self-esteem

9. Physical environment/home

10. Fun/recreation/leisure

11. Personal growth/learning/self-development

12. Others — e.g., service to others

CREATE YOUR VISION BOARD

"If you don't have a vision, you're going to be stuck in what you know. And the only thing you know is what you've already seen."
- Iyanla Vanzant

It's a picture that you create as a collage using images that connect with your most desired, most fulfilling, and happiest life. If all your dreams were fulfilled, then these are the pictures that would symbolise the life that you'd be living. I've done this many times in my life; I would sit down on the floor with old magazines and newspapers and cut out clippings of what I thought were important to me, the desires I wanted to fulfil and manifest.

Nowadays, you can use Google Images or create a Pinterest board and add all the pictures representing you living your best life. It's a fun and creative process. When you tap into your creative mind, you go beyond logic, capturing the images that visually illustrate your best life.

There was a time when I was living in Sydney, and I really wanted a red convertible. So, I found a beautiful picture from an old movie with a woman, her scarf blowing in the wind. I wanted to lose weight, so I captured images of slimmer women. I wanted to have a published book, so I got pictures of books being published. At that time in my life, I also wanted a life partner. So, I grabbed photos of weddings and engagement rings, and I put them all together. I also put a picture of a woman lying on a hammock sipping a cocktail. To me, those images symbolised being free — financially free, free in my body image, and having the free time to sit on a beach and listen to the waves whilst sipping a cocktail. All of them and then some came true. The magic, though, may sound paradoxical; I created the vision boards, then "let the desire go" because deep within, I knew that I was already blessed with or without what was on my vision board.

"What is now proved was once only imagined."
-William Blake.

Vision boarding is powerful stuff, and combining it with implicit faith and surrender is the secret. To begin, close your eyes and do the centring that we learned in the first chapter. Orient yourself and decide where the future is for you in your mind's eye, and where is the past? We all perceive time differently; some of us see the future in front of us. Some of us may see it to the left, to the right, but internally with your eyes closed, if I asked you to step in the direction of your future, which way would you go? Once you know that, then with your eyes closed, travel through time and journey into the future. See yourself moving three years, four years, five years down the line. Notice yourself living the best you, having mastered your life. What do you see around you? What are people saying to you? What are you being congratulated for? What are you sensing? What are you listening to? What are you experiencing? Capture these images, bring yourself back here, and create a visual representation of your best life.

Some of us are not quite sure what we want, but we know the feelings we want — so look for pictures and images or thoughts and ideas that invoke the emotions you yearn for. If an image has "charge" or energy for you, it makes you emotional, even if you're not sure why just capture it. Your heart and soul may be selecting and not your mind. Later, ask yourself what these pictures mean to you. You will find that you may continue to change the images as you learn more about who you are and what you want.

It may have seemed childish, but we just used a complex cognitive process - imagination, where our feelings, experiences from the past, present and unmanifested future collided, rearranged themselves, and found new connections and creative expressions in our thoughts.

We just visualised and defined what your best life would look like if you were living each spoke of that wheel at a nine or ten. You have now created a vision board to express your best life in images. In a while, we're going to look at the wheel of life again. But this time, we will look at each spoke and see where we are now. Not where we'd love to be — but where we are right now!

"Imagination is the beginning of creation. You imagine what you desire, you will what you imagine, and at last, you create what you will."
-George Bernard Shaw

If you remember, in the first chapter, we looked at the OAR model: the observer that you are drives the actions, and then you create specific results in your life. We want to look at those results. We don't want to look at them with judgment, shame, or guilt. No, we just want to look at them with honesty, acceptance, and compassion. We always do the best that we can, so we want to look at these outcomes in our lives in detail to see. Because awareness is vital. You can't change, and you can't transform what you can't see, so we want to be able to see clearly.

Take a few moments. Bring up the wheel of life again; you'll find it in the workbook and on the resource page (https://maltibhojwani.com/myl.html). This time look at each spoke and honestly give it a rating from zero to ten to represent where you are right now — then write a few words next to each rating. So, if you rated two out of ten, perhaps in health, then just write a few words about why. If you rated three out of ten in finance, explain why you felt that way. Your results will reveal the observer you are and your beliefs — not only the helpful ones but also the potentially limiting beliefs you have in each of these areas. Beliefs are powerful. The placebo effect demonstrates it so clearly when in clinical tests. Even the patients taking the "empty" pills but told they were getting the actual medication for their particular condition showed improvement. The placebo caused pain to disappear, lumps to shrink, and even hair to grow. It was the patient's belief in the treatment that caused it to work. Your current wheel of life will reveal the beliefs that you have subscribed to up to now.

In his groundbreaking book The Biology of Beliefs, Bruce H. Lipton, Ph.D ., explains that your life is a printout of your belief programming because ninety-five per cent of your outcomes are coming from that program. When you look at your current wheel of life, you will see the printout of the beliefs operating you till now. It can be quite confronting to take ownership of your life results. But it's also empowering. If you created it, you can recreate it and recreate it.

Continuing from our inherited belief systems, from the third trimester of conception till the time that we're almost seven years old, the brain is functioning at low EEG (electroencephalogram) levels or brainwaves. That level is called "theta." Theta can be simply described as a hypnotic state where suggestions get easily ingrained and stored. In the later chapters, we will explore different brainwaves when we explore meditation and how to rewire the subconscious, but for now, let's just talk about theta. When a child is young, they're operating at theta most of the time. Imagine a computer that doesn't have much software apart from the basics. The baby is downloading through observation. In our younger years, we observe our parents, caretakers, teachers and their behaviours and reactions to our actions. Keep in mind that the people we're watching were also operating from their inherent belief systems. We watch their faces and listen to their voices and tones to learn for the first time what behaviours will help us get our needs met. A subtle facial expression or missing smile from a parent may send out a message to the child that they are not loved. The young child is "writing" beliefs around how to best get their need for belonging, love, connection, and safety met — all of this is getting downloaded just through observation, which forms our core beliefs. And those core beliefs run our behaviours.

I have been a junkie of self-help stuff, books, and workshops, and I have attended so many of them in the last two decades. I tried to change my behaviours, set goals, and powerful intentions to change my life. With the beauty of hindsight, I can now look back at what truly transformed my life. I was able to see that I had deeply rooted, unhelpful, and outdated beliefs that needed to be reframed into empowering ones. The beliefs we were born with and formed in our younger years predispose us to specific behaviours - our behaviours are driven by our thoughts and subconscious beliefs. I transformed my life when I shifted some of my most unhelpful root perspectives.

This book does not have any quick fixes or easy tricks. It's a journey, and it requires us to build layer upon layer of learning, insights, and realisations; through that, we practice and practice. From repetition, practice, and commitment, we can slowly rewire our brains — that's called neuroplasticity, which is the good news. We can rewire our brains so that we can start operating on a new operating system. In the later chapters, I will share with you every-thing that I've done, built upon each other, to rewire my brain. And if I can do it, so can you.

If you want to determine what the unhelpful beliefs running your life up to now are, just look at the areas of your life that you consider suboptimal. There will undoubtedly be deeply rooted per-spectives and assumptions that are keeping you stuck. We call them "potentially limiting beliefs" or "underlying automatic commitments." These are promises that we made to ourselves when we were young just to stay alive.

Let me share a simple example to demonstrate what I mean. The first time you got a scolding from a parent for demanding their attention, a belief like "It is never the right time" or "I am not that important" or "I am not loved" might have started to get programmed into your brain.

Or perhaps you were laughed at in school for calling out an incorrect answer to the teacher's question. This might have formed beliefs like "Only speak up when you are one hundred per cent sure you are right" or "I am not smart enough" or "It's safer to be quiet." Subscribing to these types of beliefs when we were young may have been a coping mechanism to stay "safe." We learned that if we kept quiet, we could avoid getting into trouble. Well-meaning parents, myself included, unintentionally chip away at our kids' self-confidence when we offer feedback on how they can be better, installing the "I'm not good enough" program.

Let me also share an example of how such a belief that we unconsciously subscribed to as a child may be limiting us now. Have you ever found yourself in a meeting hesitating to voice your opinion, not speaking up, thinking inside, "I'm not good enough"? Or "I'm not senior enough, my opinion may be too immature" even though consciously you know that you had something to offer?

Look at your wheel of life. If you look at the areas that you've rated at an eight or nine or ten, then that means you have some very empowering and helpful beliefs in those areas. See if you can articulate some of your beliefs in those areas. They may not be that easy to find, but it would be helpful to know what they are, so you can leverage them even more to help the other areas of your life. With the areas that you scored lower than eight, see if you can identify some of the beliefs you have in those areas. It's only by learning how we can rewire our old, outdated operating systems that we can truly transform our lives. Think about it as updating the operating system so that it can cope in these new times and support you as you live your purpose and the life of your dreams. Trust that all your helpful beliefs will not be lost, they may get further upgrades, but the system will only rewrite the "unhelpful" files.

HOMEWORK

Create a vision board, keeping your purpose in mind, keeping the wheel of life at a nine or ten in mind. What are the images that symbolise you are living your best life? And then, do a reality check. Look at the print-out of your beliefs that have been running you up till now. And this time, look at it with the honesty of where you are now. On a scale of zero to ten, how would you rate your current state for each of the twelve spokes?

If you'd like to do more work on your current state, then look at each spoke and define what it would take to raise it from a two to a three. Or from a three to a four? Just one step. What would make it a little better?

CHAPTER 4:

WE ARE ALWAYS MAKING CHOICES

"Fall in love with the future image you have of 'you-mastering-your-life'
and living the best you. When you fall in love with life,
then life starts romancing you back."
- MB

So far, we have looked at your purpose, we looked at where you are now, and you envisioned your best life. Living in accordance with your life purpose in pursuit of your best life is, in fact living in accordance with a cosmic purpose. It was what you were put on the planet to do, to remember that life is meant to be enjoyed, not merely endured.

In this chapter, we're looking at choices — conscious and subconscious choices that we have available to us in every one of our life circumstances. We will look at the subconscious in depth later, but for now, we're going to look at "conscious choice." Human beings have conscious choice most of the time. Conscious choice requires us to be informed; we can only choose between options that we can see. So, I'm going to lay out distinctions to help you expand the observer you are so that your conscious choices are more informed. If you expand the observer, you enrichen your life.

"It is our choices, Harry
that show what we truly are far more than our abilities."
- Albus Dumbledore - J.K. Rowling, Harry Potter

Our brains, like a computer, have automatic shortcuts, premade choices deep within us that we made a long time ago that help us from moment to moment to decide. We don't think about them while we're making them. We look at something, and we know that it's right or wrong, yes or no, good or bad, like or don't like.

For example, if you decided long ago that you don't like mushrooms (I don't like mushrooms), then every time you see it on a menu, you're very quick to say no. We have these automatic choices already ingrained in our subconscious; however, consciously, we also need to have some distinctions so that we can choose.

"The oldest, shortest words — 'yes' and 'no' —
are those which require the most thought."
- Pythagoras

Let's look at distinctions so that we can see the nuances, the subtle differences between two things that seem very similar to the conscious mind but very different in the energy they carry in our subconscious minds. When we can see things clearly with more distinctions, then we can make better choices.

Every single time you say no to something, you are actually saying yes to something else. If you wrote the word "no" on a piece of paper and "yes" on the reverse side of the same sheet and held it up in front of you, notice when the no is facing outwards, the yes will be facing you. In every no, there is a yes on the reverse. Human beings don't like the word no. As children, we didn't like it when our parents said no to us about anything. We always wanted a yes. So consciously and subconsciously, we don't like to have to say no to something, and we hate it when people say no to us.

We take it as a personal rejection though they may not be "no-ing" us. They are just saying no to our request, opinion, or perspective. Similarly, when we say no to a project, it may trigger an unpleasant feeling — for example, when we say no to an assignment or task, we feel bad. We need to remember that when we say no to one thing, we are saying yes to something else. Are your outdated "should" beliefs still making you say "Yes" when you don't want to do something? Just because people make requests of you does not mean you need to acquiesce.

This chapter will help you know what you are saying yes to when you're saying no to something else.

"Hesitancy in judgment is the only true mark of the thinker."
- Dagobert D. Runes

The first distinction we'll look at is "judgment versus assessment." We are constantly judging and assessing through the lens of our beliefs. Judgment comes from a feeling that we are so right. We know what is right, what is wrong, what is good, what is bad. We become the judge and the jury, and we even hang people for having a different assessment than we do. However, the distinction is to have an assessment — to be able to look at something and see that it is different without having the energy or the negativity of judging it as good or bad.

Notice when we slip into judgment when we see someone behaving in a way that is different from our expectations, we judge them, we hang them, we crucify them without knowing where they're coming from. Remember that every human being you meet is making the best choices available to them based on their level of consciousness and awareness in that moment. We can't judge because we don't know what's going on with them. Being intelligent means being able to use your intellect so you can discern between two things. But judging comes from a different energy of making one thing wrong and another right.

Instead of judging things as good or bad, let's simply discern what is empowering and helpful versus what is disempowering and unhelpful for us. If you can have that lens, then every time you encounter a situation, this lens will help you make an informed choice. If I think this way is that helping me?

SELFISHNESS VERSUS SELF-LOVE

Self-love is taking care of yourself, keeping your needs in mind, and looking after what is important to you. Having a healthy focus on self-love and self-care and your personal preferences and choices is not being selfish. Prioritising alone time to just be with the wonderful you is not the same as being selfish. If you were all alone, with no access to fulfilling others' needs or catering to their needs, what would you do with your time? What would you eat, drink, do, read, listen to, watch? Who would you speak to? How would you enjoy your time? Carving out space for your preferences is an act of honouring yourself. Notice if you have old beliefs that make you judge yourself for choosing you. Are you still subscribing to restrictive beliefs that say you don't deserve to enjoy your life? When will you let them go?

Selfishness, however, is when you want to look after yourself at the cost and detriment of someone else. That's not what we're talking about here. Being able to love yourself is essential. If you don't love you, then how do you expect anyone else to love you?

COMPROMISING VERSUS ACCEPTING

There is definitely a place for accommodating, sharing and aligning with people we love and want to enjoy life's pleasures together with. This brings us to "compromising versus accepting." Being able to behold or welcome another human being as they are is acceptance. Compromise is a tricky word that can trigger some of us; there is good compromise and bad compromise. A good compromise is when you know that you are giving up something, some of your preferences, because you want to be in alignment and in harmony with another person, with a team, with an organisation. However, if by making this compromise, you are, in fact, still saying yes to your own personal growth, then that's good compromise.

"Bad" compromise is when you give up your tastes, your values, and what you stand for. You give up who you are, trying to change entirely just to fit in with the preferences of another — If you notice an iota of resentment start to build up within you, then you could be compromising too much. Centre yourself and assess if you do what you do out of genuine love, or are you merely trying to fulfil one of your basic needs. In which case, you will be operating from insecurity, not from love. The only way to master your life is to be authentically yourself and be open to loving and accepting others fully, inviting them through vulnerability to take you as you are too.

HUMILITY VERSUS SELF-DEPRECATION

"True knowledge exists in knowing that you know nothing."
- Socrates

When given a compliment, instead of saying thank you, smiling and receiving it, so many of us go, "Oh, no, no, no, that wasn't me," and we try to deflect. If you receive a compliment, accept it with an open heart, and you can still be humble. Humility is knowing that you haven't gotten "there" yet, but you're getting better and better every day and in every way. You're evolving as a human being. You know your strengths. You know what you're good at, you're aware of all the challenges in your life that you can look back on as the gifts and opportunities they were, yet you're humbled that you have so much more to learn. You can practice so much more and become even more evolved. That's why we call it mastering your life.

"Pride may be allowed to this or that degree
else a man cannot keep up his dignity."
- John Selden

Self-deprecation is when we put ourselves down. When we judge others as better than us, we put them on a pedestal and ourselves in the pit. Doing that is not going to help anyone. We need to live our strengths out loud so that others can depend on us. And that requires us to have some pride. And this brings me to pride versus arrogance. Distinctions again! We need pride — self-pride is powerful and necessary for healthy self-esteem. However, when we think that we have done something that we see as commendable, it makes us better and others lesser. We decide that other people are less important than we are. That's arrogance – and people will smell the insecurity that hides beneath it. On the other hand, pride is a sense of satisfaction for what we have done or how far we have come, and we congratulate and celebrate ourselves. Notice the nuance between pride and arrogance.

"The only thing more dangerous than ignorance is arrogance."
- Albert Einstein

None of us got here alone. I have not climbed mountains yet, but I know that those who have climbed Everest had a couple thousand Sherpas to make it possible. We never get anywhere alone; we've always had support. Gratitude is when you feel grateful for what the Universe, what God, what life has given you. You look at your life circumstances, and you feel blessed and a sense of gratefulness, thankfulness, and appreciation. Don't ever confuse gratitude with indebtedness. Feeling indebted causes us to behave out of guilt and obligation. When will you relinquish yourself from these debts?

If we've received help and support from someone, acknowledge it, be grateful for it, but know at that time that person also needed to give to us. Haven't we had times in our lives when we have been the ones to give and when we were the recipients of gratitude from others? Notice when you expect people to be indebted to you and consciously cancel that thought. Similarly, notice when you put yourself down to feel as if you are forever indebted to someone and also cancel that thought — you are not! You are grateful, thankful, and appreciative.

WANTING VERSUS COMMITTING

"Commitment is what transforms a promise into a reality."
- Abraham Lincoln

Either you are committed to doing something, or you are not. When we are committed, we don't give up. Despite trying many times and perhaps failing, we give it our all. Many of us often use the word "try" to create an out. Be conscious of when you use the word "try" to give yourself excuses and reasons. When we keep persisting at a goal, we "die trying."

When you say things like I want to exercise, I want to eat healthily, I want to be a more compassionate person. You may be using weaker words than commitment because you want to allow yourself wiggle room. Hence, if you are truly committed to something, and if it's related to your purpose, your goals, and your future self, then say "Yes" to it. Saying "Yes" is making a promise, a commitment. Don't just try a few times and give up.

Commit! Make commitments to yourself and keep them. Be trustworthy with yourself. Don't you trust people who keep their promises? Do that with yourself! Do you know how much more predictable (in a good way) life would be if you knew that you could trust yourself, that every time you made a commitment to yourself, you would keep it?

When we want something with all our hearts and commit to having it, it will be ours. Nothing can get in our way. But when we just wish and want, then we're just fantasising, and we actually know deep inside that it's not going to happen.

I believe that hope gets us through so many of life's challenges. I also believe that it is powerful to "set our hopes high," which is the polar opposite of what common culture perpetuates. The important thing is that we don't just hope, wish, and want but also commit to taking action. Surrender the desire, have implicit faith, and stay committed to what we say we so want.

ACTION VERSUS DELAY

"Inaction breeds doubt and fear. Action breeds confidence and courage.
If you want to conquer fear, do not sit home and think about it.
Go out and get busy."
- Dale Carnegie

How often do you wake up in the morning and start to delay and pro- crastinate? You have a project that you are supposed to do, and you've committed to yourself that you will do it today, but when the day starts, you think, "Another coffee, let me eat something first, let me do that first." Later. Has "later" ever been a favourite word of yours or, better yet ", tomorrow"? Delaying is procrastination. We delay simply to postpone action. Honestly, action is what keeps us in motion.

Have you had mornings when you were going to go for a walk, but you hesitate? We can hesitate for a whole morning, and then we'll say, "It's too late, it's too hot, I'll go later." This is what delay does to us; it allows us to delay further and further. If you can catch it and choose action versus delay, put on those shoes and just go before you can let that mind of yours stop you, then off you go. Once you get into something deeply, you start to enjoy it, and then your brain is in alpha, and time flies. And the next thing you know, you've had a nice long walk, or you've finished that assignment that you'd procras- tinated for so long.

How many of you want to be loved? Wanting to be loved versus loving. Again, two distinctions. Love is an energy that makes the world go round. Loving energy is the opposite of fear energy. Do you find yourself seeking love from others? Demanding love from others? Waiting for love from others? Love is not a commodity that's going to run out. In fact, the more loving you are, the more love will come into your life, and the more love you will have. You will love for no reason without expecting anything in return. That is true love; however, waiting to be loved, demanding love and attention will only push people away. Love that wants to own and possess gets jealous, and obsessive is not love. Love wants the other to have what they want.

"D-love or deficiency-love refers to a kind of grasping, possessive love. In this state, we cling to the loved one out of desperate dependency and see the loved one as a means to fill some kind of deficiency in ourselves. B-love or being-love reflects a love based on full acceptance of the other person. In B-love, we love other people simply for who they are and not for what they can do for us."
- Abraham Maslow

FEAR, the acronym that has been used a lot, is "false evidence appearing real." "Appearing", meaning the observer perceives it as real. Fear lives in the past or in the future; it is not in the present because right now, both you and I have no real fears — we're alive, fine, we're okay. Courage is the willingness to accept the pain that may come from getting hurt, being rejected, failing, being blamed, or embarrassed. When we can really accept the potential pain and realise that we will still be okay, we free ourselves from the shackles of fear.

"Courage is not the absence of fear but rather the assessment that something else is more important than fear."
- Franklin D. Roosevelt

Other flavours of fear are anxiety, worry, challenges, and concerns that what we need in the future we might not have. Or we are remembering the past, some fearful event that may not even have been our own story; we heard something that happened to someone else, and we just hold on to that fear.

Fears come from a perception or appearance that some of our basic needs may not be met. This is the perfect place for me to bring us back to Maslow's Hierarchy of Needs. At the very bottom, he's got physiological and safety — let's call them survival needs — then the need to belong and then self-esteem followed by self-actualisation. According to Maslow, human beings are motivated to get our needs met: survival, belonging, self-esteem, and self-actualisation.

So, what are survival needs? Back in caveman times, it was about staying alive, getting fed, and keeping ourselves safe from predators and the environment. Most of our core fears are linked to the basic need to stay alive not just individually but also to prevent our species' extinction.

Next come our Love and Belonging needs — to know that we belong to a tribe or a community so that we can survive. Think of a lion; even a mighty lion stands little chance when he has been ousted from his pride. He has to go and find a new pride. Otherwise, he will become prey to the hyenas.

What are the chances of survival for a person who does not belong to a community or tribe? Do they go up or down? They go down, making us extremely sensitive to any threat of being ostracised. The social pain system may have piggybacked onto the physical pain system during our evolution and are connected to the same neural circuitry.

Neuroscience research found in fMRIs, Functional magnetic resonance imaging or functional MRI shows that the same areas of the brain become activated when we experience social rejection as when we experience physical pain. The fear of being banished or exiled can feel like a "social death penalty". A breakup is described as an excruciating pain in the chest. Even linguistically, we link physical and emotional pain saying our hearts have been "broken" - 'A pain by any name' (rejection, exclusion, ostracism) really do 'hurt the same.'

After Survival and Belonging come, our Self-Esteem needs. Now that we belong, this layer of needs is when we seek respect and external validation, we want to feel validated for our strengths and uniqueness, but for it to stick, we need to internally accept ourselves for who we are. This is when we start to yearn for authentic living when we realise that we may have been "faking it" just to belong. According to Maslow, only after our survival, belonging, and self-esteem needs have been met can a human being self-actualise.

This is when we start to question the meaning of our existence and think about how we can make a difference in the world. How can we be of service? Here we are at the cusp of transcending survival consciousness.

Change begins at the end of your comfort zone – and courage sits at the edge.

Remember that each of us was born with an instinct to transcend and include. Coming back to survival in caveman times, it was about staying alive and keeping safe from whatever could attack us. So, what are these basic needs perceived as in modern times? What is survival to you right now? Intrinsically, for many of us, the survival need is met when we know that we have enough, e.g., enough money, a roof over our head, the ability to put food on the table for our families. Belonging: that we have a community, friends, people to love, to be seen. The need to be seen is part of both our self-esteem and belonging needs. Self-esteem: that we feel good enough, valuable, that we are of contribution, and we bring value to the communities and society in which we live. Notice that all three of these needs are very intrinsically linked. We need to feel worthy, to feel like we belong, to feel that we can survive.

That's why we use the acronym "false evidence appearing real" for fear because it's not about whether they've been met or not. It's about our perception — the observer that we are in that moment having a sense that these needs are being met or not being met. And when we are operating from a perception that our needs may not be met, we overcompensate, over-index, and over-focus on survival, belonging, and self-esteem. This is when we become insecure — a lack of feeling secure. Our behaviours are driven by the observer we are, how we perceive our values, needs, thoughts, and feelings.

If we are continually operating automatically from unreal perceptions that our needs may not be met, how do you think we will behave? Those behaviours will become self-sabotaging, and we will play out like self-fulfilling prophecies. Think of someone you may have met know who was so desperate for money that every interaction with them smelled greedy and needy. Desperation for love comes across as demanding and constantly expecting something from another. Or on the other extreme, they become doormats conforming to fit in, losing themselves completely. Someone with low self-esteem comes across as arrogant, showing-off to overcompensate for that lack of self-worth, and it will most likely push us away. No one wants to be around someone who's demanding love from them. Or someone who is overly insecure. Or someone who comes across as always being competitive, mistrusting, or greedy. Can you see that paradoxically, if you operate and behave from the fear that your needs might not be met, then that fear will, in fact, keep you from getting those very needs met?

I've been there, so I know. There was a time in my life when I was struggling so much to get my survival, belonging, and self-esteem needs met that no one wanted to be around me. I just wasn't aware of how I was coming across. I was exuding low energy, which repelled people who resonated on higher wavelengths. All that your heart desires and soul yearns for vibrate at high frequencies. An analogy to understand this is to see "Joy", "Love", and "Abundance" vibrating along a high orbit. If we want to welcome more of that in our lives, our consciousness needs to rise and resonate at that elevated level – we can't "pull" the good-stuff down to lower frequencies; we need to rise up to attract it into our lives.

Based on the work of David R. Hawkins, M.D., Ph.D. in his book Power versus Force, the lowest frequencies are shame and guilt. Often, they come accompanied with blame. Do you still have memories of the past that make you feel ashamed? Are you still feeling guilty about some of the choices that you've made? Do you still blame others or judge them for some of the choices that they've made?

These low, horrible feelings may have served you in some way in your life journey, but now they have become shackles, and it's time to break free and let go. We can stop carrying them with us by taking responsibility for our part, accepting that we can't change the past and consciously choosing to forgive.

You cannot master your life and live in victimhood simultaneously because you are a victim when you're blaming and shaming. Expressing dissatisfaction about everything you experience is perpetuating your victim mentality.

A Course in Miracles (ACIM), also referred to as the Course, co-created by Helen Schucman and William ("Bill") Thetford and published in book form in 1976, consists of 365 lessons based on the underlying premise that the greatest miracle of all is the act of simply gaining a full awareness of love's (read God's) presence in our lives. It is the awakening to the realisation that we are not separate from God.

Lessons 69, "My grievances hide the light of the world in me", through to Lesson 78, "Let miracles replace all grievances", focusses on what I feel is the essence of life mastery.

According to the Cambridge dictionary, grievances are defined as "When we have a complaint or a strong feeling that we have been treated unfairly". Well, first up, life isn't fair. It is tipped in your favour when you see through the film of blame and worry.

When we complain, we believe that things "should" be different, which is futile. Worrying about how much worse things could get is wasting precious energy that could be channelled instead towards what we want. Everything we desire is beyond the "eclipse" of our grievances. When I finally dropped partaking in drama and catastrophising my life situations, I felt peace and freedom.

I had broken beliefs that ranged from two extremes of entitlement to worthlessness, how things "should" be to "can't ever" be. I had shattered the limiting beliefs that were holding back my potential. The double whammy of beliefs is that they not only reinforced themselves by looking for more evidence to hold them in place but, at the same time, because they were so opaque, they blocked what came in unless they fit my beliefs.

Let me share this visual analogy to help in your ability to accept, forgive, and let go. Imagine you are in a small room with no windows or doors, and the walls are literally closing in on you. There's a timer in front of you displaying that you only have one minute to get out. If you do nothing, you'll be smashed. On the ground, you see three manholes with lids. You lift the lid off the first one and see sharks and crocodiles ready to grab at you, so you shut it quickly. The timer is now at 38, 37, 36 seconds and counting, and you can feel the walls coming closer. You lift the second manhole cover, and in there are scorpions, spiders, and snakes, so you shut that one as well, horrified.

You look up at the timer. 17, 16, 15 seconds left. You are feeling that fear. The walls are closing in, time is running out, and if you do nothing, you will surely die. You lift the lid off the third one to see a sewer — smelly, turbid, putrid, but shallow. So you know that if you jump in there, you may survive. You shut it as well because it stinks, and you can't bear the smell. But the timer is now at 10, 9, 8 seconds left. Moment of truth. What do you do?

What do you think I would do in that circumstance? Yes, I would lift the lid to the sewer and jump in. Unless you are an ophiophilist or selachimorphaphile (lover of reptiles and sharks), I'm pretty sure you'd do the same. I've been in many metaphorical manhole situations in my life, and I know that I've always chosen life. The moment after I jumped in, what do you think I would exclaim? Yay, I'm alive! Do you think I'd be aware of the smell? No. I'd just be happy to be alive. I shared this analogy with you to help you see that each of us in all of our circumstances always choose the best option available to us at that time based on our awareness and consciousness. Based on the observer, we were. Remember this even if you've disappointed someone or hurt someone who really matters to you. You chose the only option that you could have. (On the resource page, you will find an audio-visual version of this manhole analogy.)

As you find yourself swimming in the smelly sewage water, when you've forgotten how you ended up there, you start to wonder, what am I doing in these waters? Why have I created this? This is when you may feel regret, shame, blame, and even guilt.

And the people looking at you may have their opinions, which could hurt. Why is Malti swimming in those waters? Why did she choose this? Why did she do that? When "they" comment on your choices, remember that they have no clue of the options available to you at that time; only you do.

Lower versus Higher Vibration States

- Judgment vs. Assessment

- Selfishness vs. Self-Love

- Compromising vs. Accepting

- Self-deprecation vs. Humility

- Arrogance vs. Pride

- Indebtedness vs. Gratitude

- Wanting vs. Committing

- Delay vs. Action

- Being Loved vs. Loving

- Reacting vs. Responding

- Blame vs. Responsibility

- Shame vs. Acceptance

- Guilt vs. Forgiveness

- Pleasure vs. Joy

When you can "re-write" your history, changing the context of your story to find new meaning and see a causality from your "suffering," you will have evolved in consciousness and rewired your beliefs. And empowering beliefs = a new life!

Remember this manholes story for two reasons. One, let go of shame once and for all. You might have done something that you're not proud of, but you did it. You might have hurt someone in the process, but guilt is futile. When we feel guilty, we have made an unconscious decision that we did or did not do something that we should or should not have done. We went against our values and consequently deemed ourselves as "bad people." We choose to punish ourselves by never forgiving ourselves. Guilt is what we make up so we can feel "good" again about doing something that we judged as "bad." Let me say that again, we did "x", we judged it as "bad", now we feel bad about it, "guilty", so now we can be "good" people again.

Guilt, shame, and blame became part of the old paradigm when some perhaps benevolent religious leaders felt the need to control society through reward and punishment by instilling God's fear and wrath on all who deviated. When you become the master of your life, you know that the Universe is not a punisher but is infinite love and compassion. When you subscribe to this truth, you will experience life as always being tipped in your favour even when you can't see it yet.

Two, when you feel that someone has hurt you deeply, know that they were probably not thinking of you; they were thinking about themselves, and that's okay. They chose the best option available at that time based on the observer that they were and their level of awareness and consciousness.

In hindsight, you can always look back and say I could have done this, and I could have done that; I should have done this, and I shouldn't have done that. But you could not have. Forgive your past, forgive others, and accept that we all chose the best option available to us at that time. Now, you have learned so much, you have grown so much, and you will make different choices. If you still have people you need to forgive, then forgive them because if you don't, you will be carrying these grudges, and they will come with you into your other relationships. Let go of shame. Let go of blame. Nothing needs to be anyone's "fault." Let go of guilt.

Take responsibility now. You are evolving and growing, moving up from survival and fear consciousness through transformation towards self-actualisation consciousness, which is love consciousness. Know that the next time you find yourself in a situation where it feels like you're back in a room with the walls closing in on you, you will be able to tune into your higher awareness and trust your soul's wisdom to help you see through your limiting beliefs that narrow your vision. See beyond the illusion of the limited options you perceive, for they may just be more outdated beliefs. Have faith in the potential opportunities within the seeming challenges. Trust that you will make conscious choices that are aligned with your purpose and values. Wait, be patient, and allow your inner knowing to guide you on what could be the next steps for you.

The path of mastery requires us to let go of the outdated belief that life was "happening" to us and to let go of our past mistakes.

HOW DO WE LET GO OF OUR LOW-FREQUENCY EMOTIONS?

Thoughts are the meaning that our mind gives to the presence of a feeling. Emotions are physiological states that live in parts of the brain (and body; note the body includes the brain). It is the way our brain gives meaning to bodily sensations based on our past experiences that provide us with information about the world. As children, we learned to repress many of our emotions. If you think of a pressure cooker, the lower frequency repressed, suppressed, unexpressed emotions accumulate in our psyches and bodies, building more pressure only to keep us heavy until it is released. Choosing to let go of those emotions will make us lighter to rise above, evolve from and transcend our deeply rooted old hurts.

Letting go of our own limiting beliefs and past pains have the power to heal our current relationships as well. As we become lighter, we create an environment for life to thrive in our presence through our own loving beingness. On the flip side, we often leave a relationship, job, manager, or country thinking that things will be better out there only to be deeply disappointed to find that we've created very similar circumstances just with new characters and roles. This is because the "leading man/lady," which is you, has not yet evolved enough to be in a new script.

The way to let go is to first allow ourselves to feel these old hurts and then make a conscious choice to let go. Being intentional about letting go is the way to let go. Take the time to be alone in silence and feel. Trust the wisdom of your body to know how to let go in whatever way it chooses. Some of us can let go through movement, exercise, thrashing it out in a basketball game, sports of any kind, or dance. For those who play a musical instrument, setting the intention to let go of "whatever needs to be let go of" before playing will do the job.

For some of us, splashing paint on a canvas may do the trick, and for some, writing about it may be the avenue that works best. Whichever way you go, all it requires is to have that willingness. Give yourself permission to let go. It doesn't need to be complicated. Don't expect to completely forget whatever you think brought about the emotion, as your thoughts about it are irrelevant. What you are letting go of is the underlying pressure buildup of limiting emotions.

You can set an intention to let go of your "karma" or inherited ancestral beliefs that no longer support you, by first trying to articulate what you think they might be. For me they were something along the lines of "Life is hard", "Surviving is the best I can hope for", "Money is hard to come by". If you can't pinpoint specific beliefs, it's fine too, just tune in to get to the feeling or sensation. Next, ask yourself what you think the original positive intention behind those beliefs might have been, then thank your ancestors and acknowledge their suffering and sacrifices, if it weren't for them, we wouldn't have been born. What they did, got us here, but it won't take us further in our evolution. So, thank them and then let go of the "life-sentence" with gratitude.

You will know you have successfully let go when you notice in time that the same memory of these stories no longer holds the heavy energy it once did. It can be as simple as trusting your inner wisdom to do the letting go when you sleep when you meditate. It can even happen while you are taking a long walk.

Soon after my father passed to the light, I realised that I was holding on to emotions that I directed at him, and it took time to let go of them. I used every method in the book, and when I thought I was done, something would trigger me again, and I found there was still more to accept and release. I'm blessed with an amazingly intuitive brother, Sanjay, who has been a guiding light with concise suggestions for me as I worked through my journey of letting go.

Anger is typically a secondary emotion that predisposes us to take action. It can be beneficial when we use it for positive influence. It enables us to set boundaries and say "No". Physiologically, anger causes the release of hormones like epinephrine or adrenalin into our bloodstream. This causes blood to flow to our extremities, especially our hands, so that we can "fight".

Anger, like all emotions, is not negative. They are emotions. How we express them can be more or less helpful. Underlying the anger are usually emotions like sadness, disappointment and fear. Something that we perceive as unfavourable for us happens. We decide someone else is responsible for it. We deem it unfair that someone has caused us this suffering or damage and want someone to "pay" for it.

We have beliefs that sound something like, "You did or did not do this", which equals now "I have to or can't do that", meaning "I suffer because of your actions". Can you see the relationship between Anger, Blame and Victimhood?

My anger stemmed from the remnants of the scarcity mindset that I had inherited. Even though I was living a life of abundance, I still got triggered back to low-frequency concerns around survival and money, and then that made me even angrier. What upset me was not the anger itself but that it sent me back to feeling like a victim again to others' actions. My freedom lay in reframing the equation and changing the meaning that I had unconsciously attached to my feelings.

To let go of this anger, I knew that I had to use all my faculties, head, heart, will and soul. The steps from Blame and Victim to Ownership and Mastery was Acceptance and Forgiveness. I reframed my thoughts by accepting my feelings of disappointment and sadness for what I perceived as broken commitments. I accepted that there was nothing more to do. I forgave myself and him, knowing that both good and bad things happen in life, and I welcome both with the confidence and courage that I can handle them. I meditated and prayed on this regularly until I noticed the related triggers lose their effect on me. I acknowledged my fear and reassessed that most things that happen to me are fantastic. I had nothing to be insecure about. I renewed my faith in the unknown again and became at ease with uncertainty.

To recap, bring your awareness to the feeling in your body or mind, set the intention to let go of what is no longer serving you, be willing to let go, and simply instruct yourself to let go. It will happen naturally until it is done. Over time, you will know that you have let go, your life experiences will have transformed. This will occur even if you are not consciously aware.

We've covered needs and fears by looking at Maslow's Hierarchy of Needs. Let's explore values now. The Barrett Model is the breakthrough work of Richard Barrett. Inspired by Abraham Maslow's Hierarchy of Needs and tested over more than two decades of real-world experience with thousands of organisations, the model identifies seven areas that comprise human motivations. These range from basic survival at one end to service and concern for future generations at the other. If you would like to understand it deeper from an Organization Culture perspective, visit the values centre website. The levels have since been renamed, but here I have shared both names. (https://www.valuescentre.com)

It provides a proven and handy map for understanding the values of employees, leaders, and stakeholders, and I often use this as a baseline to help my corporate clients measure, craft, track and transform the culture of their organisations.

Barrett took the tip of Maslow's hierarchy pyramid, turned it around on itself, and created a vertical bow-tie-like shape — the seven levels of consciousness model.

The levels are:

1. Viability (Survival)

2. Relationships

3. Performance (Self-Esteem)

4. Evolution (Transformation)

5. Alignment (Internal Cohesion)

6. Collaboration (Making a Difference)

7. Contribution (Service)

In the workbook and on the resource page (https://maltib-hojwani.com/myl.html), you will find a link to the personal values assessment where you can pick ten values that matter most to you right now. Once you've done the survey, you will receive an email with a visual representation of which levels your current values sit at, together with a robust coaching worksheet with questions to help you understand yourself better.

"Who you are, what you hold dear, what upsets you, and what underlies your decisions are all connected to your personal values."
- Richard Barrett

Coming back to the Barrett Model, survival, belonging, self-esteem, and self-actualisation remain almost unchanged from Maslow's levels. Barrett linked unique value words to each level, and only the first three levels include what he terms "potentially limiting values." When we operate from fear, a belief or perception that these needs may not be met, we can become controlling, micromanaging, and mistrusting others and life itself. We may behave in a "win-lose" competitive manner, and we may become boastful or complacent. The accumulated limiting values in a system — and here a system could be an individual, a team, an organisation, or a country — equals a score that Barrett coined as "the Cultural Entropy® score." This reveals the amount of energy consumed in doing unproductive or unnecessary work and the degree of dysfunction (friction and frustration) in an organism or organisation generated by the self-serving, fear-based actions of its leaders. This is also relevant for the individual. Operating as the "CEO" of our own lives, each of us have entropy that can tell us how much energy we waste on self-serving, fear-based actions that directly stem from our limiting beliefs around some of our values and needs.

Above Level Three, Barrett turns Maslow's "self-actualisation" tip over and splits it into four more levels:

Level Four is "Evolution" or "Transformation." Transformation is where you are right now. If you weren't in the transformation consciousness, you wouldn't have been attracted to a life mastery book. This is where a human being is searching for more, where we start to realise that just trying to get our needs met is not enough. At this level of consciousness, we are already more privileged than many people. With this blessing comes the awareness to be kinder, more giving, and contribute to helping to raise the consciousness of those who may be less fortunate.

Remember, Levels One, Two, and Three are needs:

1. Survival needs

2. Belonging needs

3. Self-esteem needs

If we perceive them as not being met, it leads to fear. And that fear, insecurity, anxiety, and worry will drive our behaviours. This paradigm of fear will not allow those actions and behaviours that will move you towards living the life of your dreams and mastering your life. We need to shift our internal operating system from living to get our needs met (as in living from fear) to living from love, living from purpose.

Transformation requires courage because courage is not the absence of fear. You don't need to be courageous if there's nothing to fear. Courage is knowing that something else is more important than what we fear. It's what gets us to step outside of our comfort zone and step beyond our fears. We can look at the level of Transformation as the bridge between evolving from a paradigm of fear to one of love and trust.

"Meet this transient world with neither grasping nor fear.
Trust the unfolding of life, and you will attain true serenity."
- Inspired from teachings of the Bhagavad Gita

Level Five is "Alignment", "Internal Cohesion." While I'm evolving into what I'm becoming, how do I integrate who I used to be with who I am? How do I transcend and include and be all of me? Level Five is about trust, integrity, and authenticity. To me, we access Level Five consciousness when the ego and soul reach internal alignment. I think of this as a state of consciousness where we can partner and collaborate with our soul.

Level Six is called "Collaboration", "Making a Difference." Where we want to coach, help others, and collaborate with others. We seek opportunities to make a difference in somebody else's life. It's where we know inside that just living to get our own needs met is not enough anymore. We want to make a difference. Be mindful that we can sometimes "do things for others" just to fulfil the "need to be liked" which is again a "fear-based" behaviour and a potentially limiting attribute on Level two.

Level Seven is called "Contribution", "Service." Pure service is when life is just about being of service to others. Level Seven is not "better than" One. Six is not better than Two. Barrett stressed that the model is about transcending and including integrating a healthy focus on all levels of consciousness. Hence, we need to look after our basic needs, like having our roots firmly planted into the ground, so that we can grow, evolve, transcend, and make a difference to others. It's like the seven colours of a rainbow. It's only when you have all seven colours of the spectrum that you can see the white light.

Think of a tree. Only a tree that's solidly planted in the ground can grow so that its shade and fruits can be of benefit to others. Looking after yourself is as important as wanting to serve others. The foundational levels are just as important as the higher ones. In fact, we will not feel fulfilled if we only focus on the first three, but we will not be grounded, rooted, or even reliable if we only focus on the higher levels. Like the aeroplane analogy, the stewardess always tells us to put the oxygen mask on ourselves first, and only after we are breathing well can we look around and help others.

But when we overemphasise our focus on our basic needs out of fear that they might not be met, then we become insecure, and our consciousness lowers. When our vibration is low, we cannot attract our best life, we cannot live our best life, and we cannot master our lives. We need to raise our frequencies so that we operate and attract what we want. All the "good stuff" we yearn for vibrates up high.

We were each born with an innate soul's yearning to evolve and transcend.

This is why some people who seem to have everything that others envy are still miserable, unhappy, and unfulfilled. Because they're probably not yet living their higher values, they're not living their self-actualisation needs. Human beings were not put on the planet to be alone and self-fulfilling. We cannot transcend by just looking at ourselves and trying to survive alone. Levels One, Two, and Three are "I" focused, and Levels Five, Six, and Seven are "We" focused. The only difference between illness and wellness is the "I" and the "we." Especially now, we are called to become a society that strives for a win-win instead of competition; win-lose. Because if we focus only on I, then not all of us will survive. If it's not you or I who start to operate from higher frequencies, who will make a difference in the world? You and I have Wi-Fi. We have mobile phones and electricity, which makes us more privileged and more blessed than many in the world. If we don't take inspired action to do our part in making a difference, elevate the planet's consciousness, and help people live a life of dignity to end hunger and poverty in the world, then who will? As Rabbi Hillel so aptly said, "If I am not for myself, who will be for me? And being only for myself, what am 'I'? And if not now, when?" Any little thing we can do for others, like charity, paying it forward, sharing our blessings and good fortune, will help give a little hope to others. These acts of kindness will create a snowball effect that will eventually raise the consciousness of the entire planet.

You might wonder why we should care about self-actualisation and living higher-level values in this competitive world — well, do it for your own fulfilment. In the workbook and on the resource page (https://maltibhojwani.com/myl.html), you will find links that educate you about the seventeen goals that the UN declared in the year 2000. Look at them and then think about what will fulfil you as you start to evolve as a human being. What do you care about? When we are unconscious and live our lives just struggling to get our own needs met, we end up feeling like we're in a rat race, trying to survive, trying to belong, and just trying to be seen. It's only when we start to evolve, transcend, transform, and begin to live the higher-level values that we begin to find meaning in our lives. We start to feel fulfilled and truly happy, and our needs seem to naturally take care of themselves. I often use the Seven Levels of Consciousness model with my corporate clients. As Richard Barrett so aptly puts it, "Organisations don't transform; people do." The close link between the entropy score going down and the performance indicators or "results" going up is notable. It brings home the truth that the leaders' level of consciousness will attract, retain, and grow the very people right for the organisation they are trying to build.

REACTING VERSUS RESPONDING

Reacting is automatic. Look at the word "re-act" — all we're doing is acting again, something that we have so deeply ingrained in our psyche. Reactions are like a knee jerk. Reactions are human because they keep us alive when we need them to. Think about yourself walking down the street, and there's a bus coming at you. You don't want to stop and think about it or start assessing, "Oh, I wonder how fast this bus is going." No, you need an automatic reaction that moves you to get out of the way so that you can stay alive.

Those reactions come from a part of our autonomic nervous system, mainly the amygdala — a set of almond-shaped neurons at the back of our brains. Together, they keep us alive in times of danger. The amygdala is always on the lookout in the peripheral for danger. Whenever it picks up a potential threat, something that smells, looks, feels, seems dangerous to our survival, the amygdala will hijack our thinking brain so that we get out of harm's way by reflex.

The last thing we need in these instances is our neo-cortex to think about what to do. There is no time for that. That's why this knee jerk reaction is called the amygdala hijack. Our blood, adrenaline, and cortisol rush through our system, going to our extremities to trigger our fear response: either fight, flight, or freeze. In animals, fight is when they attack, their claws come out or they "show their teeth", with us humans we tense up ready to fight or shout. Flight is when we run away or withdraw. And freeze is like a deer in headlights; with us, we stiffen almost unable to respond or move.

Most of the time, we don't encounter rattlesnakes in our modern lives, and we're not faced with buses about to hit us. We have regular day-to-day situations: we hear the phone beep, we get a particular email, we see someone's name show up, a child spills milk, but unfortunately, the amygdala causes us to react as if our very survival was being threatened. Have you ever been in a situation where you wish you hadn't done or said what you did when you look back on it? Or you wish you had said something, but you didn't because you froze? Or someone was speaking to you in a dominant tone, and you ran away, or perhaps you fought back, and you were rude.

It's like a dumb policeman or a smoke alarm that's over-sensitive. This means that even if it's not a fire, it hijacks your thinking brain, you lose your mind, you literally go nuts, and you react. Often, the behaviour is not according to your values or goals or with helping to strengthen our relationships. Usually, you look back, feel bad, and wish you hadn't said that or sent that email.

We do have choice. When we become more self-aware of what upsets and triggers our amygdala, we can take a breath, and we can choose. And in our choice lies our freedom.

When we notice the amygdala hijack's onset, we need to push the breaks by slowing our autonomic system down consciously. Breath is the only function of the ANS (autonomic nervous system) that we can intentionally alter. We slow down our breathing, which in turn slows down our heart rate, blood pressure and calms us down. Then, we have a window to change our thoughts.

Remember I said that the amygdala hijacks the thinking brain? Well, here is when we need to "kickstart" and "reboot" it. The surest way to do so is by asking ourselves helpful questions. The neocortex was designed to answer questions when asked, so when we ask ourselves something, we will be switching our brain from automatic (Amygdala reaction) to manual. Think of when we apply the brakes on a speeding car. We learnt to push the pedal to the floor repeatedly until the wheels stop. Similarly, when hijacked, we may need to pose multiple questions to ourselves to help calm us down to make helpful choices.

We do not have the right to just blow off automatically, relying on old subconscious habits to get our needs met. And we do not need to be victims of our life circumstances. With distinction and awareness, we can respond by making conscious choices that are in accordance with our purpose and living our best lives. I wish I knew this twenty years ago when I was so very feisty and volatile. This simple knowledge is one of the most critical life skills we all should have. I was so impressed with modern education systems when I learnt from my daughter, a schoolteacher, that simple brain science, including the amygdala's function, mindfulness and breathing exercises to help kids calm down, is being taught to eight-year-olds!

"Between a stimulus and response, there is a space, and in that space is our freedom to choose. And in our choice lies our freedom and our growth. Choice. That's the advantage, the blessing, and the responsibility that we as human beings have — to be able to choose."
- Viktor E. Frankl

PLEASURE VERSUS JOY

Pleasure comes from external stimuli usually experienced through the five senses that make us feel transiently good. Often the things that give us pleasure are emblems to memories of the past that we have associated with joy and happiness. For example: seeing firecrackers, the popping of a champagne bottle, certain songs, looking at an object of beauty, or getting a whiff of a fragrance that reconnects us to moments of beholding joy.

In our pursuit of joy and happiness, we seek out and indulge in what we can derive pleasure from, especially when our desired life — that is, firing on ten on all the spokes in our wheel of life — seems far away. The word "enjoy" comes from "en" and "joy" and means to give and receive joy - fully. Enjoying the juice of life and its many pleasures is our birthright but be mindful that what we habitually choose to indulge in may actually be taking us away from what we know will offer us true joy and deeper fulfilment. Habits get reinforced because of the perceived reward we get from "indulging". Instead of rewarding ourselves with pleasure from, say, alcohol, food or shopping, we could use the self-pride and self-celebration we often feel when we stick to our commitments as reward enough. Habits are automatic behavioural patterns that started with a decision we made in the past often to attain pleasure or stay away from pain; check if any of these "decisions" around enjoyment are still true for you. Think of the three joyful memories you used to craft your two-word purpose and notice your own distinction between pleasure and joy.

We know that letting go of lower-frequency fear-fueled emotions is imperative to living a joyful life, so when we indulge in short-term pleasures, we must check to see if we could be slowing down our "letting go" process. Guilt, anger, sadness, and shame can accumulate and build pressure if we continuously suppress them through distractions like TV shows, alcohol, or food.

If you know on some level that you are trying to suppress or retreat from your emotions, then you may want to reconsider your "pleasure-givers" to check that you are indeed indulging for enjoyable albeit transient endorphin rushes and not as a way to suppress any discomfort.

The only way to truly let go is to feel these emotions, however uncomfortable. As they say, the only way out is through. So, indulge, eat, make love, drink, dance, and do all the things that you enjoy, but do them with the underlying energy of enjoyment, the awareness of choice, and the wisdom of transience. Indulge guiltlessly, trusting that your inner wisdom will guide you on when to stop. Simultaneously, invest in your long-term happiness by committing to what you know is aligned with your purpose, for that investment will have much higher returns than life's little pleasures.

CHAPTER 5:
CHANGING YOUR MIND —LITERALLY

This chapter is the heart of transformation. All we've been doing up till now has been priming you for this very moment. You are halfway there. You found your purpose in two words that connected with joy. You looked at your wheel of life, noticed where you are now, and visualised where you'd love to be and what living your best life would look like. You looked at your basic human needs and saw how your fears are deeply connected to those needs.

We established three core fears, and they are linked to the need for survival, belonging, and self-esteem. Fundamentally, we realised that these fears of not having enough, not being liked enough, or not being good enough come from a perception of needs — note "perception" not being met. We also realised that we have an innate need to self-actualise. And if we're not living that need, if we're not looking for purpose and meaning in our lives, trying to make a difference in the world, then we feel unfulfilled, no matter how satisfied our basic needs are.

Now it's time to look at how we can literally change our minds. Changing our minds is about looking at the subconscious. Understanding what has been driving our behaviours up till now. What are those habitual thought patterns and belief systems that are so deeply ingrained in us that have created all the outcomes that we have in our lives? How do we intervene and reprogram, update and upgrade that subconscious system that's been running our lives? Are you ready to change your mind?

Human beings have choice. In the previous chapter, we looked at distinctions so that we can make informed choices consciously. Unfortunately, what is driving us most of the time is our subconscious mind, our beliefs. We know that we were born with some beliefs already as "factory settings" from our ancestors. We downloaded the rest of our programming in our younger years and then, through repetition, habit, and validation, they became stronger and stronger. Many of these beliefs are incredibly helpful; they create "fast-thinking," which is needed to function. But coming back to mastering your life and living the life you want — the one that you visualised — will require you to shift your limiting beliefs.

What are the beliefs that you have right now that are not helping you? Look at your wheel of life again and at the areas where you feel you're not living at a nine or ten. Underneath those outcomes are the belief systems that have been playing out your life against your conscious intentions.

How many of you have read countless self-help books, attended workshops, and spoken to professionals, and yet despite your efforts, you still find yourself stuck in that hamster wheel, still creating very similar, disempowering outcomes in your lives? It is because your subconscious has been running your behaviours, and you can't have new results when you are unconsciously committed to your old beliefs.

Let me give you a funny example. Recently, we were moving the furniture around in our house. We had this really thick rug; it was so thick that we got used to always taking a step up before we approached that rug to not trip on it. We moved that rug to a different part of the living room, but weeks later, every time I walked past that part of my living room, I unconsciously stepped up even though there was no rug there anymore to trip over. Do you see how we form habits mentally, emotionally, and physiologically in our bodies?

"Your beliefs become your thoughts, your thoughts become your words, your words become your actions, your actions become your habits, your habits become your values, your values become your destiny."
- Mahatma Gandhi

Change your mind, and you literally change your life. How do we change our minds? Physiologically change our minds? The brain is an organ, and the mind is a series of all our thoughts. If we can change our thinking, reprogram our minds, then we form new neuropathways and will behave in new ways and surely create new outcomes in our lives.

Let's look at the potentially limiting beliefs that many of us may have. You were born with some already "downloaded" into you from your genes and ancestors, and you subscribed to some of them growing up, just like you might subscribe to an email list. But now, you can consciously select which beliefs you want to continue to subscribe to and which ones you want to permanently unsubscribe from! In the workbook and the resource page (https://maltibhojwani.com/myl.html), you will find a list of many limiting beliefs to explore and check which ones you might have unintentionally and unconsciously subscribed to.

When I was a young girl growing up, we were very comfortable; we lived in a fabulous condominium in Singapore's poshest districts. I was oblivious about how privileged we were. I remember one day, my dad and mom were arguing in the room. My mom was crying, and I didn't understand why. Dad came out angry, yelling at my brother and me that we couldn't turn on the air conditioner anymore. The air conditioner, seriously? Of course, I didn't realise then that he was struggling financially and needed to cut corners. This was soon followed by the house being put on the market, our belongings stuffed into boxes, our pet Pomeranian Snoopy-the third being sold off, and us migrating overseas almost overnight. At that young age, I formed a belief that if I wanted air conditioning, if I wanted the simple pleasures in life or any kind of stability, if I didn't want to feel loss, I would have to get it or do it myself. "I can't rely on anyone to give me what I need." Can you see how this belief is no longer logical? But it was what a little girl formed in her mind before logic could intervene. Then I went through my life, obviously reinforcing that belief. I continued to attract situations where I couldn't depend on anyone if I wanted anything. Fast forward many years later, when my marriage ended, I found myself stuck in survival mode with that same broken record playing in my head: "I can't rely on anyone." "I have to do it to myself." "I don't deserve to be happy." "I don't deserve to be in a healthy relationship". I realise now that I was unconsciously drawn to quotes to "back" my beliefs. Being a literature student, I loved the classics. From The Mayor of Casterbridge by Thomas Hardy, there was one line that I always held closely: "Happiness was but the occasional episode in a general drama of pain." It took me half my life to replace this ridiculous conditioning with "My default setting is pure joy; suffering is a choice" in order to break the curse of drama and pain that I had unwittingly cast upon myself.

Now these beliefs weren't all bad. They made me very independent and gave me that theme song that "I will survive." And I did. My life was always about survival. Just in time, just enough, just in time, just enough. There was never more than enough. I was living with a very strong belief system that I couldn't rely on others, that I would never be successful, and that I would never have abundance in my life. And even after all the "work" I had done on myself, my upgraded belief was still extremely limiting, I want from utter hopeless to all I could hope for, all I deserved was "just enough, just in time". Can you see how disempowering these beliefs were for me? I spent nights and days praying, begging, and wishing for life to change. But the thing is that when you pray desperately, then what you're actually saying is that you don't deserve it; you don't expect it. You don't believe that you can really ever have it. Become aware of your beliefs even when you pray.

People say seeing is believing, but I say believing is seeing. It was only when I was able to shift my beliefs and start believing that I was worthy, capable, and that I could rely on others, trust others, and have a life of joy and abundance that I started to see slivers of it finally appear in my life. With each glimpse, I believed even more, and then it grew and grew, and it completely transformed my life.

"No problem can be solved from the same level of
consciousness that created it."
- Albert Einstein

I had reached the stage when I realised that just enough, just in time, and just living to survive, belong, and be seen as good enough was no longer enough for me. I had a deep yearning to make a difference. That's when I started writing and coaching. However, the old beliefs were still running me.

Independence is awesome. Being able to survive is commendable. But it wasn't enough. It served me up to a certain point. It got me here — but what got you here isn't going to get you to where you want to be; it isn't going to take you to mastering your life. I mentally "tuned-out" of that frequency, just like we do to change radio-stations and I reframed my beliefs to "I am worthy," "Together, when I collaborate with others and trust others, I can make a bigger difference in the world." "I deserve to be happy" And slowly, my life started to change. Similarly, you need to shift your beliefs, change stations. I still have many beliefs that I'm sure are not empowering, but all I need to do is look at the symptoms in my life that will show me what those beliefs are.

When you're faced with moments that upset you, situations that you're not happy with, or results and outcomes in your life that you don't think are what you originally intended, check for the beliefs that are running them. I even look at physiological symptoms. Anything that shows up in my health is giving me a signal or a clue to some belief that is not serving me anymore.

Let's pinpoint some of these potentially limiting beliefs that you might have. The first one I want to talk about is the "should." Many of us have these "stereotypical shoulds" running our lives. There are gender-bias "shoulds" For example, "You should be a good girl," "You should please others," "You should help others," "You should be of service," "You should cater to everyone's needs," "You should put others before you." Or, "You should provide," "You should never cry," "You should be strong all the time," "You should never show weakness." Can you see these as beliefs and not as truths?

"Nothing that is possible in spirit is impossible in flesh and blood.
Nothing that man can think is impossible.
Nothing that man can imagine is impossible of realisation."

"The brain does not make the man; the man makes the brain."
- Wallace D. Wattles

Many of these stereotypical beliefs no longer serve us; they are in fact disempowering. Look for your "shoulds" and then look for generalised statements that you used to believe were true. You may want to challenge those beliefs because many of them are not valid, and they are not true. You can either be right about your beliefs, or you can be happy and master your lives. Your choice! The thing is, being right even of our limiting beliefs can feel very good. "You see I was right; you can't trust anyone.", "life is hard!" Wrong and strong is what I call it, but it doesn't help us.

"Whatever the mind of man can conceive and believe it can achieve."
- Napoleon Hill, Think and Grow Rich

When we let go of deeply held beliefs about the world, ourselves, and what is and isn't possible, we open up our lives to limitless possibilities.

Because these beliefs were formed before we could even conceptualise or add logic to them, many of them don't really make sense. But we've believed them to be true; they're deeply ingrained and cannot be altered through the conscious mind alone. That's why our best intentions are often not carried out as we're working against the grain of the underlying beliefs that were etched in to "keep us safe."

These beliefs need to be reprogrammed in the subconscious, so how do we do that?

Let me share a bit about brainwaves. The four we will explore here are: beta, alpha, theta, and delta.

Beta is when we are talking and thinking logically; we spend most of our time in beta. The next level, called alpha, is when we relax a little, when we are very focused on one thing. Alpha is where children up to the age of six spend most of their time. (Read the book The Biology of Beliefs by Bruce H. Lipton, Ph.D to learn more.) The next time you call your child while they are deeply engrossed in a game of Lego, don't get upset when they don't respond. It's not that they're being stubborn; they are in alpha, and they literally can't hear you. I'm sure you've had that experience as well where you're so engrossed in something that you don't even realise where the time went. That's alpha.

The next level is called theta. Here we access memories, creativity, and where "the pieces come together" like a jigsaw puzzle falling into place. It's when you have great insights and realisations; where things just make sense.

The subtlest brain frequency is delta: deep relaxation where we can access our intuition, where we know without knowing how we know. Haven't you had moments in your life when you just had a feeling, and you knew — you just knew something, but if anyone asked you how you knew, you wouldn't be able to explain it? You couldn't use your logical mind to explain your inner knowing. Haven't you also realised that when you went with that inner knowing, things worked out better? They were more synchronous? Don't you wish that you were able to have the confidence to trust that gut instinct and that inner knowing more frequently rather than allowing your busy beta mind to talk you out of it through the logic of what seems possible and what doesn't?

That was a brief overview of our brainwaves. I'm sharing this with you because when we were young, we were in this hypnotic state, which is theta, when we were getting programmed. So, in order to reprogram our beliefs, in order to literally change our mind, we need to deliberately access theta, weed out our limiting beliefs, and plant more empowering, supportive beliefs in their place. And in time, when you are ready, you won't need more beliefs because Truth with a capital T will be guiding you. In other words, when we are in a hypnotic state, that's where we can reprogram our minds. There has been extensive research and work done in this area, by many including Bruce H. Lipton, Ph.D and Mike Dooley to name a few who have hugely influenced my life.

We need to reprogram the subconscious beliefs that are not serving us. But how do we do that? I don't care how electricity works or how it makes its way into my home, but I'm happy to know that if I turn on a switch, the room lights up. Similarly, through the research, the dedication, the perseverance, and the hard work that has been invested in this work by so many experts, I trust them and resonate with their teachings, and I am sharing with you what has worked for me.

The first and most powerful way to achieve this is through meditation. Having a frequent, committed practice twice a day to meditation is profoundly powerful. It's the key to transformation. I will attribute my entire life transformation in the last ten years to when I started to meditate. Meditation is the bridge with the ever-present Divine Grace. It was what I could do to remember that all I needed was to be – that the love of the Universe is always within me.

When I entered my forties, I knew that something was still missing in my life and my work for profound transformation to occur. I knew that I was missing sacred knowledge. My intuition kept telling me to explore meditation, but I had formed a bias against it. When I was younger, the only ways I knew of learning meditation was by becoming a disciple of a guru and abiding by their rules. I resisted being "initiated" vehemently as it went against my core value of freedom. I felt that my community imposed it upon me as a prerequisite to belong.

So, when the niggling impulse to learn meditation returned, I attracted TM – Transcendental Meditation into my life. I appreciated the practical teaching backed with science research. I also had a great teacher who held it with lightness.

Why does meditation work? Because when we meditate, we dip into our purest essence. Our brainwaves go down from beta to alpha to theta to delta, dipping into pure consciousness where the magic happens. When we meditate, we give our minds the time and opportunity to relax into the slower frequencies of theta and delta.

Meditation is available for all of us, and it's easy to do. We just need to bust all those myths about how it should feel and accept that it is indeed so simple that we make it difficult for ourselves. There are many forms available. I practice a form of meditation that started out as TM, Transcendental Meditation. For TM, you need to find a teacher, and you can find a local one on the tm.org website or from my resource page.

We're very lucky nowadays because there are so many free apps you can download. The one I like best is called Muse. Muse comes with a headband. And when you use the headband, you'll be able to visually see your personal experience of the brainwaves that I explained earlier.

I now practice and teach The Dynamic Mind Practice™(DMP). It was introduced to me by my teacher Gita Bellin. I committed over eighteen months of my life to her Facilitator Development Program™(FDP) and am privileged to have been able to learn the art of facilitation directly from her. We had four residential weeks in the United Kingdom and two in the Emirates. Little did I realise how personally transformational it was going to be for me.

Having been a meditator myself for many years before meeting Gita, and knowing fully well that we can only truly transform with Divine Grace, I always wanted to be able to teach meditation, to whisper "the gift of silence" into the ears of people who came into my world. Gita's meticulous detail and precision put into teaching DMP was profound, and I most appreciated how the tradition and lineage of this ancient wisdom were honoured.

The DMP is a deep relaxation mindfulness practice. You can learn DMP directly from Gita through the Dynamic Mind Practice App. The app contains detailed videos that explain the various brain-waves emitted throughout the course of our day that we heard about earlier and how the practice assists us with profound stress release. It also has an advanced skill for enabling a complete, deep and unin-terrupted night's sleep. I am an accredited teacher of DMP, down-load the app and learn from Gita, then join my free live sessions by registering on my website, where I will assist you with any follow-up questions you may have.

I want to distinguish between the two types of meditation that I practice. There is pure, silent meditation, and there are guided med-itations to reprogram our beliefs.

With pure, silent meditation, you do not set an end goal; in fact, if you're searching for something, or you're trying to achieve some-thing through your meditation, it is counterintuitive to meditation.

Pure meditation is effortless. And it's not about control; you're not trying to "get" anywhere.

> *"Through Transcendental Meditation, the human brain can experience that level of intelligence which is an ocean of all knowledge, energy, intelligence, and bliss."*
> *- Maharishi Mahesh Yogi*

Even though I explained the brainwaves and frequencies earlier, you can't go into a meditation expecting to go to the lower frequencies. In fact, if you try to force it or control it, the subtler states will elude you. Because then you are going back up into beta. Pure meditation is to just sit humbly and quietly, allowing the meditation to meditate you. It's an easy, effortless focus on the breath or on a mantra. Sitting diligently twice a day for fifteen to twenty minutes and simply meditating. Not attaching any fear or "should" to it — just making it a thing I do daily, accepting thoughts, letting them flow, and gently coming back to a mantra or breath naturally. This sort of meditation is what changed my life.

With committed, daily practice, we become more peaceful as we (re)connect with pure consciousness on a regular basis whilst simultaneously releasing old stress. You could think about it as a "weeding out" process. Life starts to flow. It becomes synchronised. That's been my direct experience with meditation of this sort. This type of meditation helps to release stress. Some people refer to the release of our deeply rooted stress as releasing old karma. Think of this as stirring the bottom of the ocean where silt has accumulated over time even before this lifetime. These could include generational trauma that our ancestors experienced and passed down to us through our DNA. The amygdala hijacks we explored earlier are linked to these deeply rooted stresses and beliefs we've formed. As we release and release and release, we are able to live a much more peaceful, connected life of unity, of oneness, of wholeness. Electroencephalography (EEG) and Functional magnetic resonance imaging (fMRI) have shown that regular meditation reduces the activity in the amygdala, and in doing so, our pre-frontal cortex – also referred to as the "CEO" of our brains in charge of decision-making and higher-order brain functions becomes stronger.

The second type of "meditation" that I also practice is to specifically rewire my belief systems. To me, these are not really meditations; these are hypnotism in a way. Here, we are guided into a slower brain wave state, and at theta, suggestions are made in the form of affirmations. We deliberately hypnotise ourselves to plant and program new belief systems. Reprograming the subconscious helps us live in alignment with what we want rather than live based on the old beliefs that are outdated and unhelpful.

They are two different methods, and my personal recommendation is to do both. Do the pure meditation, and over time, you won't need to plant or hypnotise anything because then you will be living in accordance with nature. In the meantime, do the hypnotic types of meditation to help you rewire your brain so that you are operating from a newly upgraded operating system. I hope this is clear. In the workbook and on the resource page (https://maltibho-jwani.com/myl.html), you will find more explanations and links.

Another way to reprogram your subconscious is through a repetition of affirmations.

I deliberately stressed the letting go of limiting beliefs from our programming before mentioning affirmations because if we come back to the analogy of planting seeds, using affirmations or positive thinking when we have multiple core beliefs in place that are still limiting us is like planting new seeds in soil that's already full of weeds but expecting these affirmations to flourish. We can though work at this from both ends where on one end we meditate, let go, and weed out the soil whilst on the other end, we plant affirmations.

Picking a few affirmations that are powerful and repeating them to yourself, especially when you're just about to fall asleep, when you just wake up, if you happen to wake up in middle of the night, when you're having a shower, when you're exercising, when you're drawing or colouring — those are the times in your day when you are naturally in theta. This is when we are in theta's hypnotised state where the gates are wide open for you to create and expect what you want in your mind. Plant these affirmations at those times repetitively, and you will start to create new neural pathways.

Roger Ballard, who wrote a book called The Way of the Carrot, talked about using the writing of powerful suggestions by hand to rewire the subconscious. And I was inspired by one in particular: "I continue to allow love, life, and abundance into my life." It's powerful because it's about opening the valve by allowing. I wrote it by hand every single morning, a full page of "I continue to allow love, life, and abundance into my life." The objective is not to keep the pages and read them again but just to get the hand repeating the affirmation. From the mind to the hand to the mind to the hand, this repetitive practice naturally slows down our brainwaves whilst simultaneously creating new neural pathways in our minds.

Listening to affirmations when you're in theta, including sleep meditations, are extremely powerful, and the one I use is Kelly Howell's "The Secret Universal Mind."

An abundance affirmation that I memorised by heart and still repeat in my mind often is "Money comes to me from multiple sources in increasing quantities on a consistent basis," (inspired by Wallace D. Wattles, Bob Proctor, and Napoleon Hill). This anchors the truth that money is indeed limitless energy, and all we need to do is believe that abundance is infinite to magnetise it into our realities. "Every bite and sip I enjoy keeps me in perfect health and shape." "Every day and in every way, I am getting healthier and healthier." "I love myself, body and soul." All of these affirmations help keep me in great shape. Another one I repeat consistently is "Dear God, please come and express yourself clearly through me." This helps me step out of the way especially when I am coaching, writing, facilitating workshops, and speaking. It helps me allow for truth to be channeled through me. It helps me let go of my ego or my showing off what I know and trust that what needs to be heard by the system will flow through me clearly. Script your own affirmations or use the ones I have shared to help reprogram your mind to believe in truth.

Changing the things that you smell also has a deep impact on your subconscious. I have found that scents can trigger the subconscious to open up and welcome many blessings that are intrinsically already "ours for the taking," but it's only our own veils of limiting beliefs that prevent them from having a clear channel to flow through us. This is why deliberately smelling certain scents can help to rewire the subconscious.

Another funny story comes from when I first tried this essential oil called Abundance by Young Living. When I was first introduced to it by a dear friend, I didn't like the smell. My body was resisting the smell that was associated with Abundance. Why? Because I wasn't worthy of abundance. I didn't think I deserved it. I wasn't open to it. It was only after a while when I started doing everything else to reprogram my subconscious that the smell started to grow on me. And now I love it so much that I diffuse it at home daily. Money truly started to find new ways to come to me: from glistening coins appearing on the ground, unexpected tax refund cheques in the mail, and gifts including a brand-new laptop when I needed one, to free flight upgrades and nights in seven-star resort hotels. I even received a huge windfall that was the maximum amount possible through a company policy terminated a year later with me as its only benefactor.

Use every single method that you can think of — the ones I'm sharing with you, the ones in the workbook on the resource page (https://maltibhojwani.com/myl.html), and ones that you will discover yourself. It is quite a unique journey because you're looking for resonance. What might resonate for me may not resonate for you.

It's a profound process, and you need to treat it with gentleness and reverence. It's a sacred thing to do — to consciously reprogram your subconscious mind — but once you do it, then imagine this: ninety-five percent of the time when you're being run on autopilot, your autonomic nervous system, your subconscious will be running what you want it to run. It will be running through your highest purpose, your desires, wants, and goals. You will be living from truly mastering your life rather than from the old belief systems, which were to the tunes of "I don't have enough," "I'll never have enough," "I'm not good enough," and "I'm not worthy enough." Now what would you rather have running your life?

One of the highest frequency emotions that you can feel is gratitude. Taking the time to journal or to think about what you're grateful for every single day will force you to look at life through the constant lens of gratefulness and gratitude, which will raise your own vibration. When you are vibrating gratitude, you will attract more things to be grateful for. It's like magic. Pausing to appreciate the beauty of God's creation in the scent and symmetry of a flower or the intense colours of a peacock's feather is gratitude.

"Sincere, heartfelt appreciation is pure love and is the strongest message to the Universe that this is more of what you want to experience. Feel grateful and attract more reason to be grateful for. It works like magic." - MB

As it took your entire life to ingrain all the limiting beliefs into your subconscious, it may take a bit of time and commitment from you to reprogram it. And that's why you need to bring some practices and rituals into your life. Initially, you may need to make yourself do them, but slowly, they will start to become habits. Repetition builds will-power, and you will find that forming a new thinking habit in one area of your life will strengthen your will and support the other parts of your life. When you start to feel uncomfortable on the days that you do not express gratitude, meditate, or listen to something inspiring, you will have made these rituals your new habits.

Once your rituals become habits, they become more and more accessible to you, and slowly, after a lot of conscious repetition, they will become your new operating system. When we have a thought associated with our old limiting beliefs, and we consciously practice our new higher frequency thoughts, new neuro-networks in our brains are activated. Myelin is the insulation of these networks, think of myelin as the coating on a network cable's fibres. The more we mindfully practise a new way of thinking, the more myelin will insulate the circuit, making it more robust.

Hebbian theory by Donald Hebb often summarised as "Neurons that fire together wire together" suggests that through repetition, we can make the connections between the neural synapses grow stronger.

We may have our old ways of thinking deeply ingrained in us, but through repeated mindful practise, we pave new paths for the old impulses, giving ourselves the choice to go up the empowering "newly-paved walkway" instead of down the old unhelpful "dirt-road".

You will notice yourself "catching" your thoughts, reframing instantly, and making better choices. Don't be disheartened though because your old operating system is still there, and especially when you're stressed, or when you're challenged, your old voice may come back and say to you that you're not worthy, you're not good enough.

This is where you use conscious choice again to bring back the new practices and rituals. And tell yourself that, hey, that's no longer true. Use words like "cancel" or "delete" to quickly reframe your thoughts. There are many other modalities out there — you could go for hypnosis, you could explore EFT, you could explore psychK, the Silva method, and a myriad of other healing methods. Once you know that you indeed can reprogram your potentially limiting beliefs, you will find the ways that work best for you and pick the ones that resonate with you. Books, videos, and programs will come to your awareness as if by magic since you will be resonating on the frequency of truth, and you will just know which ones to pick up and which to let be.

"THOUGHTS BECOME THINGS... CHOOSE THE GOOD ONES!® - MIKE DOOLEY

An important distinction I hadn't explained earlier is "faith vs. doubt." Faith and doubt cannot coexist. One drop of doubt is enough to completely remove faith. Notice when you think of what you want and try to trust and have faith that it will come, but then you have this doubt creeping in, and then it doesn't happen? One iota of doubt is enough to derail it all. You need to train yourself to have faith regardless of whether you see results or not. Do not give up. Know that we often give up moments before the magic.

I worked out every day for almost two and a half months, but I saw no results. I did not give up; I just kept going. Persistence, commitment, giving it your all, and having the faith that it will be — that is half the battle won. We need to stay the course. Don't let doubt come in and take any of your faith away. Think of doubt as a drop of dye in water. It will change the colour of the water completely. Stay in trust. When you pray, pray from faith. Expect and believe that it will come, and if not, then something better, always better. When you visualise, picture it from what you want, what feels joyful, rather than from what you want to fix and don't allow the "buts" or the "ifs" of your pragmatic, practical mind to mar the vision of your best life.

"Worrying is like praying for what you don't want to happen," said Maharishi Mahesh Yogi, the founder of Transcendental Meditation. I love that quote, and if you're a parent, stop worrying about your children because all you're doing is praying for the very thing that you don't want to happen to them. Always visualise what you do want. Visualise the highest good for all instead of worrying. Instead of trying to mitigate the risks, have faith and expect more good. When we pray to God or the Universe to prevent what we don't want to happen, it presupposes a belief that we are not worthy and deserving of all the joy that is indeed ours. I believe that blessings are super powerful especially when they are for the people in our own ancestral lineage, so as a parent or loved one, the most powerful thought we can have for humanity is to visualise the best for all. Stop worrying the worst! Start envisioning the best!

This chapter has included profound sacred truths that work. But they don't work by simply listening to or reading about them. You need to do the work. You need to commit to meditation, affirmations, writing by hand, to any modality that you can think of to help you rewire your beliefs. When you change your mind, you change your life. Simply put, we are "changing our brains" by "learning" new thinking habits, so that when we find ourselves at the juncture where our old habitual thoughts that had powerful neuronal connections, could have run us, we are now able to reroute the impulses to go where we want them to instead.

We may sometimes slip and have thoughts that are not helpful. A worry, an anxious thought, a limiting thought, a negative thought. When you do, all you need to do is notice it; you're now aware. Don't let it run on autopilot. Notice it, and the minute you do, cancel it — say it in your mind or say it out loud — cancel, cancel, cancel, or delete, delete, delete. You could even use your hand and wipe it away. What you're doing is instilling the habit of noticing when you are saying things from autopilot that are no longer in alignment with the life of mastery that you so want to live. When you are saying or thinking things that are low in frequency, the opposite of what you want to manifest is being attracted to you.

> *"If you realised how powerful your thoughts are,*
> *you would never think a negative thought."*
> *- Peace Pilgrim*

But if you catch yourself and pause in the moment, then say anything else that will help you cancel it, you can reframe it instantly in your mind, "play the desired track," and think or say something in a much more positive, higher-vibration way. Soon, you will become so used to cancelling that you will eventually stop saying things that are not helpful. You'll have a "kind watchman" constantly on the vigilant lookout to catch it when you say a phrase that is not aligned and not coherent with your higher vibrations and with attracting and living the life that you so desire.

*"Your desired life already exists beyond this dimension
of time and space; you've dreamed it into creation all your life.
You don't need to re-create it. You only need to believe
and vibrate at the same frequency and resonate with it."- MB*

CHAPTER 6:

GOING WITHIN
WITH MEDITATION

Have you had a chance to come to one of my live sessions? Well, if you haven't, then please register. Have you downloaded a meditation app on your phone? If not, I urge you to do so. In this chapter, I will address many of the frequently asked questions that I get about meditation. I have addressed them solely from my perspective, sharing my personal experiences and my knowledge of meditation.

By this point, I'm sure you've realised that living a path of mastery is going to take some focus and energy to truly create the life of your dreams. You might also think that it will require willpower, but the thing about willpower is that it takes energy, and when does willpower go away or weaken? When our energy level is down.

"The energy of the mind is the essence of life."
- Aristotle

Willpower drops when our energy drops, and the only way to have more energy in your life is to nourish yourself better. For our body, we nourish ourselves with good food and exercise. What do we do for the mind? We need good sleep, but most of us are not getting good enough sleep every night of the week. Meditation is almost like plugging yourself into a power source of infinite energy so that you can live a vibrant life full of vitality!

I am a huge advocate for meditation and attribute most of my transformation, my life successes, and my joy to having started a meditation practice in my life. People say that we need to be lucky in order to live the life of our dreams. What's the relationship between luck and meditation? When we meditate, we dip into pure consciousness — it's that simple, and the truth is that the purpose of life is to be joyful. God, your higher self, the Universe, the field of the collective consciousness, divinity, or whichever name you prefer to use for Truth is indeed all love. It's our essential nature to be in joy and to relish life, but we have formed so many limiting beliefs that cloud this truth and make joy elusive. Meditation allows us to dip beneath the crap and bathe in truth emerging more connected to the Source. This is when we experience that perfect storm in our lives again and again and again. Everything is as it needs to be, and we live in synchronicity with life.

Synchronicity is linked to our intuition, and we can only access that gut instinct when we relax, when our brains drop into theta and delta frequencies. When you meditate, you experience that deep relaxation more and more frequently, making you ultimately more intuitive. And when you're more intuitive, you make choices coming from your intuition, not just from logic, and that's when synchronicity has the opportunity to manifest in your life.

WHAT DOES LUCK HAVE TO DO WITH IT?

"When you develop and trust your intuition, you tend to take only inspired actions and realise you're manifesting the life beyond your dreams when things seem to fall into place at the right time — synchronicity. This phenomenon is perceived as good luck." - MB

If you want to be luckier, happier, and have more energy, then meditate. Most of us are not hermits. We don't want to renounce this world and go live in the mountains. We could do that and meditate 24/7, but that's not what most of us are looking for in this lifetime. Many of us want to be able to live in this dimension, enjoy life, have creativity, innovation, partnerships, relationships, even achievements, have a sense of power and dignity, and enjoy everything that life has to offer. And we also want to evolve spiritually.

We want to have both, which requires integration. Going away on a retreat for two weeks and meditating is great, but many of us have an intense experience only to come back to a day-to-day life and forget about it; very few of us really continue the practice after coming back to our lives. What I'm talking about here is having a daily practice integrated into your daily life where you're also going about doing the things you need to do, leading the businesses or the companies you do, doing the jobs that you want as well as giving that time and space to your spiritual connection. What then starts to happen is that you live in this plane, in this life, but you are very much in connection with the essence of who you are at the same time. You sense that oneness within whilst having the separate experience of your unique human experience.

I often get asked the question that "I can't seem to meditate, I feel restless, I get impatient, and I have a lot of random thoughts. I find myself thinking about work, thinking about my shopping list, thinking about what I'm going to do next. I find myself thinking, and then I don't think I'm doing it right." Well, the good news is there is no right or wrong meditation. Do not berate yourself and do not judge your meditation.

Every meditation is a good meditation. And every meditation includes thoughts. Expecting to have no thoughts is elusive; you cannot tell yourself not to have thoughts and at the same time be "thoughtless." It's not about doing; it's about being and allowing the mind to flow in its natural tendencies. It is effortless, and it is easy, and it requires no concentration and no control. "Take it as it comes" in the words of Maharishi Mahesh Yogi, the founder of Transcendental Meditation upon which many meditation apps and teachings are based. Swinging like a pendulum from your thoughts to a light focus on your breath or a mantra is the process of meditating.

It is normal for thoughts to be experienced when we are releasing stress. Think of stress as energy, and when energy is released, our minds can't accept the "energy" without associating images, words, and ideas to it – so the energy release is experienced as thoughts. In fact, if you have thoughts, that's great. It's just more and more evidence that you are releasing stress. Restlessness is normal. Our minds are not accustomed to sitting down and doing nothing. We human beings have been so accustomed to doing so much in ten minutes. We have so many activities that we do in short periods of time that "just" sitting for ten or fifteen minutes makes us restless because we think that we need to be productive.

If that's how you feel, you probably need to meditate even more. All you're going to do is give your mind the opportunity to chill, to go, "Phew, thank you. I really needed that." So let go of your restlessness by letting yourself just be. It is the best investment of your time you will ever make. Then at the end of your practice, take a quiet moment, give thanks, and sit silently to let the experience settle in and install. And then you can get up and get on with the rest of your day.

Another question I get asked a lot is "I have no time to do anything, and you want me to sit twice a day for fifteen to twenty minutes? Where am I going to find the time?"

Well, if you meditate, you will start to notice that you'll become more productive, more creative, more intuitive. Things will start to flow in your life, synchronicities will happen, and then fundamentally, you will be saving time. The ROI is intangibly immense.

"But how do I meditate?" You just sit. It doesn't have to be cross-legged. You do not have to be in any particular pose. As long as you're comfortable, keep your back straight, don't lie down as you may fall asleep, but sit almost anywhere — even on a train or a plane; in your car in a car park even if it's noisy in your surroundings. Once you close your eyes and start to bring your focus inward, you will become less sensitive to the noises around you — and trust me, you can be in your own little bubble for a while anywhere.

Wouldn't that be a breath of fresh air in your life to have some time of silence wherever you are? "But how do I know it's working for me?" I can only speak from my personal experience. Don't expect the mystical to happen to prove that meditation "is working" for you. Don't expect to have hallucinations or any kind of magical phenomena. Don't make that the goal. If you have an experience that felt magical, good for you. Give thanks for it, but don't search for it. Meditation is ordinary. How you assess whether meditation is working for you is not during the meditation, but it's how your life pans out after you meditate. Give it about a week or two, then just look around at your life, at your mental and emotional state, and notice how you're reacting to life's many circumstances. When you start to have more and more coincidences in your life, and life seems to just work, when life seems to be romancing you back, then you can be sure the meditation is working.

Many people ask if they have to change their lifestyle, become vegetarian, vegan, stop drinking alcohol, etc. Well, the answer is no. I resisted many religious sects and communities in my younger years because of these types of imposed restrictions. I fell in love with Transcendental Meditation and later with the Dynamic Mind Practice because there were no restrictions on my lifestyle.

The interesting thing though is that through repetitive and regular practice, you tend to become a little more sensitive to things that don't support your meditative practice. But please don't worry. You don't need to give anything up. The only thing you need to do is sit twice a day. If you feel you don't have enough time to sit twice a day, or you can't see enough benefit or value, then sit once a day. If you can't sit once a day, then sit once every two days. All I am saying is that some meditation is better than no meditation, but it takes your personal experience in feeling the value and benefit for yourself to become a believer and to prioritise meditation above the other things you do in your day.

"Take it as it comes and take it with ease." Don't turn it into another "should" that you have to do in your life. Because once it has the should energy, then you will be doing it just to check a box. Your life will flow with ease when you meditate because you want to, because you enjoy it, and because it's blissful. It has to come from love. Not from fear. If you start thinking, "Oh, if I don't meditate, then bad things are going to happen to me," that's counterproductive to the message of life mastery. Life is not working against you; it's working with you. All you need to do is let go and flow with life.

Who is it for? I've taught meditation to kids above the age of twelve, CEOs of large global organisations as well as founders of start-ups, executives, entrepreneurs, artists, housewives, fellow coaches, almost anyone. Meditation is for anyone. It gives you more energy. We can never win the battle with time; all of us have twenty-four hours in a day last I checked and seven days in a week, so all we can do is manage our energy better. And what better way than to meditate?

I have some interesting stories to share about my experiences in teaching meditation. One company that I worked with converted a room in their office into a meditation room. Another one actually turned some of the tiles on the carpet to represent meditation so that it would be a reminder. I've heard from many of my clients who have had their children and colleagues tell them to please go meditate because they had noticed from the way they were behaving that they didn't get in the quiet time that day that made them a better person to be around.

I invite you to find your own practice, download an app, learn Transcendental Meditation from a teacher, learn any form of meditation that you resonate with, or join me on one of my live sessions.

MASTERING YOUR LIFE THROUGH MEDITATION

To summarise, when we meditate, we experience deeper states of consciousness, the stillness at the bottom of the ocean of our minds. In order to be in these deeper levels of consciousness, we need to cross the bridge between our conscious mind and our subconscious mind. In the many methods of meditation that I have talked about, there are techniques to cross that bridge easily, effortlessly, and quickly.

The reason to meditate is to experience the merging with pure consciousness, the universal mind, your soul, your true essence, your

God-self — frequently. This is when you choose to "lose your mind" full of incessant thoughts in order to find your Soul. In the process of meditating, you release the daily stresses that accumulate and gradually your deeply held stresses of the past. These stressors have kept your amygdala hyperactive and hypervigilant, always looking for the next thing to react to out of fear. Instead of living from the emergency mind of fear — of fight, flight, and freeze — the reactive mind — if we keep our practice of frequent meditation, we can raise our consciousness and literally rewire our brains to operate from choice and from love.

Living a life of mastery is raising our state of consciousness and living from love, kindness, gratitude, awe, and with a sense of humour so that we can be compassionate to all living things. Instead of reacting to life, we become "responsible" — as in - we have "the ability to respond" to life.

CHAPTER 7:
TAKING INSPIRED ACTION

Even when you're unsure of what the next step could be.

"God provides the wind, but man must raise the sails."
- St. Augustine

On this journey together of mastering your life, we are now coming out of the internal work that we've been doing over the last few chapters. If you visualise an iceberg where only the tip is above the water but what lies beneath is gigantic, your behaviours and actions are above the water, at the tip. All that we've been doing leading up to this moment has been below the water level in self-awareness.

As you start to feel that stirring, and wonder where all this is going and want to see some tangible results in your reality to show that you have indeed started to make some progress, it is the ripe time to come back up, to surface above the water level to take action. It is the space between the inner work and the outer that leads to taking inspired action. We have been approaching it, bottom-up and top-down.

Think back to when you discovered your two-word purpose that connected to moments of joy and meaning from your life. Imagine if all your actions came from within, from your purpose, from your values, from your deeper levels of consciousness, your spiritual purpose?

Imagine if everyone was living by radiating their life purposes. That's taking inspired action. It's pausing in the moment, reconnecting with what really matters to you, your higher self, and then choosing to act from there. The world would be so beautiful if each of us radiated that light through our actions.

Although I say that we're going to take action and that we want to make magic happen, it only truly shows up in our lives when we come from a space of gratitude. And gratitude is when you can look back at your wheel of life, at every part of your life, from acceptance and knowing that actually everything is already perfect. We already have everything that we need. I know this can sound contradictory because we're saying we are already living mastery, but then we're also saying we want more. We get more fulfilment from life when we start to see the perfection of where we already are — when we can look back at all our past experiences from gratitude, whether they were difficult, challenging, or joyful — and see how we coped and grew from them to get us to where we are right now.

Having said that, taking action is essential to growth. We live in this world, in this plane, where things happen when we take action. Taking inspired action means that we don't just take it from our mind; we don't just look at opportunities from a strategic point of view, but we trust our knowing and trust our gut. Through self-awareness and spiritual practices like meditation, journaling, affirmation, and expressing gratitude, we start to feel the stirring within us. It inspires us to do something, to bring it forth into our reality.

I like to use the analogy of planting. Lately, I've developed an interest in gardening. I've started to grow flowers on my balcony. I've got jasmine, gardenia, tuberose, you name it — if it can grow in Singapore, I'm starting to grow them. But with planting, as with life, as with manifesting our desires, we need to put in the first effort of finding those seeds, saplings or bulbs and putting them into the soil, and then we need to be able to balance nourishing with letting go. We water the plant, make sure it's getting enough sunlight, prune it, and pull out the weeds. There's a lot of love and devotion that goes into it. In Hindu scriptures, the word "Tapasya" essentially means devotion for the sake of devotion. You're not looking at the plant and saying, hey, grow, grow, grow. It doesn't work that way. We have to let go. We do our part. And we stay in awe and in gratitude as we see it do its own thing. Beholding its awesomeness.

As the saplings start to grow, as the shoots begin to emerge from the soil, I look at them with amazement. When they flower and bloom, and I smell the fragrance, I willingly receive the joy that comes from all this growth. And when I accept it and acknowledge it with awesomeness and gratitude, it only gives me more.

Similarly, with our lives, anything that we want to create requires us to put in that effort, that energy, that action, that planting of seeds. What are some of the seeds that you will plant in your career, in your business, in your entrepreneurship, in your relationships, in your health? What seeds do you want to nourish more instead of wasting that energy on harbouring limiting thoughts?

When I think of how I got to where I am today, I am in the space of utter gratitude; I'm thriving. There are so many people in my life who have helped to cultivate the soil in which I have been able to thrive. Of course, that's relationships. I trusted them, and I also contributed to their lives, and they continued to cultivate the field in which I was able to thrive in my uniqueness. Same for you. Look around at your relationships. Who in your life is cultivating that soil for you to thrive in? As I reflect with gratitude on all the beautiful coincidences and synchronicities that have happened in my life, I realise that I had a part in them as well. I planted the seeds professionally. I said yes to almost every opportunity that came my way, trusting my intuition, of course, but if it felt right, even if I didn't logically know how I was going to do it, I would say yes.

When I wanted to write, I wrote to almost one hundred different publications. This was before the internet was popular, so they had to be print publications. I wrote articles and articles. I approached professors in my fields of interest, wrote research articles, and submitted my articles to magazines. When I was lucky, I received replies, primarily rejections. Most of the time, I just never heard back from them. But it didn't stop me. In fact, I got even more motivated. And I love to quote from Thomas Edison's teachings — how many attempts did it take before he invented the light bulb?

"Our greatest weakness lies in giving up. The most certain way to succeed is always to try just one more time." "I haven't failed — I've just found 10,000 ways that won't work." - Thomas Edison

Every failed attempt wasn't an absolute failure. It was actually a different iteration that got him closer and closer to a better answer. But he had to tweak, he had to iterate, and he had to keep going. So remember, when you sometimes feel like giving up, you could possibly be at that cusp where it is about to manifest. It's like pulling out the plant from its roots just because you can't see the flowers yet. You might have pulled it up just before it was going to give you its first bloom.

I didn't give up. I kept submitting my articles. And finally, I received a letter in the post that said yes, we love your article, and we'd like to publish it. Somehow that started to snowball, and another magazine said we'd like to print. We'd like to translate it into several languages. And that's what gave birth to my career as an author. Then I was approached by producers who wanted to make a TV show of thirteen life coaching episodes back when I was in Sydney. I was thrilled and started to write it, but a few months down the line, they cancelled the whole program when I was almost finished. I was slightly disappointed, but I didn't give up. Then in one of my past supposedly "failed" relationships, I had met someone who introduced me to a publisher, and I said, "Yeah, well, you know, I've written all this already. It was meant to be a TV show, but have a look at it and tell me what you think." Lo and behold, they came back and said we would love to publish your book. And that was my first book called Don't Think of a Blue Ball.

By then, I had instilled an attitude of gratitude. When I shared this with my publishers, they asked me to create a journal called TAG - Thankfulness, Appreciation, and Gratitude. Then I remembered the magazine that had translated my article into several languages, making me wonder if perhaps my book could be translated as well. Hence, I approached publishers in Indonesia, which led to my first book being translated into Bahasa, becoming Buat Apa Susah.

I'm not telling you all this to show off or boast, and I apologise in advance if that's how it's coming through, but my intention to share these wins and these losses is to show you the number of attempts behind every perceived success. There were so many attempts and so many failures, but they weren't failures.

From the books came my first invitation to run a program including workshops and coaching for the most senior "C-suite" team of a global conglomerate. I didn't know how to do workshops. I was a coach, I worked with individuals, and I had never worked in the corporate world, but I said, "Yes." I hadn't a clue of how to do it, but I said yes because something in me said, "It's not going to be easy. It's terrifying. But I'm ready, and I'm willing to try." After accepting, I reached out to my whole network of friends, helpful, kind souls who wanted to see me thrive. Some invited me to observe their workshops, giving me tips. They taught me and groomed me, so I was equipped to do my first workshop. Trust me, when I walked in there, I was literally shaking. I was so intimidated. But then I remembered centring.

So I made an excuse, went to the bathroom. And I sat there and did the exact centring that I shared in this book. I breathed into the centre of my body, accepted my emotions, and at that time, my heart was pounding. I said it's okay to feel this way. This fear, it will pass. And then I listened to the voices in my head that were saying you're not good enough, go in there, say that you're not ready, and just run away. But then I continued to sit with my eyes closed, my breath slowly calming down, "No, I'm going to listen to the calm beneath the chaos. I'm going to listen to the silence beneath the sounds." And I found my centre. I stepped into my worthiness, and I trusted that as I am here and not anyone else, then it's because I am meant to be here and not anyone else - with these souls here today. So what if they are senior executives? They are but human.

So I went in. I let go of my need to look good or prove myself, trusted my instinct, and took inspired action. I dropped my agenda, listened to the group, and I allowed wisdom to flow through me. After that first workshop, I became more confident. That led to me running multiple programs and later attracting some of the most inspiring clients and consultancy firms that I collaborate with today. All the companies I work with have purposes that go beyond profit.

Apart from my career, my personal health also transformed. I've shared that I used to be obese, and then I lost some weight, but I always had extra kilos on me. Recently, I was so dedicated, exercising every day, sometimes twice a day, watching my food, taking my supplements, visualising, and doing everything that I ask you to do, but I didn't see any results. Every time I got on the scales, I just saw a fluctuation of zero-point-five kilos up or down; no results. In those moments, we want to give up, saying to ourselves this is so much work, and it's not working. What am I doing? What's the point?

But something in me said, you know what, I can accept myself the way I am. But I also know that I will feel more confident, and I will feel more authentic if I can show myself that I can stick to it and truly achieve what I set out to achieve. So, I stayed committed, tweaked my program, sought out more support but stuck to it. And slowly, results started to show, and the scales gave me evidence that I was shedding the kilos. My clothes fit again. That renewed confidence from seeing results was like seeing the little shoots start to grow on a plant. That's when we feel confident, and life gives us these little gifts when we persist when we have faith.

Relationships can heal if we put our heart into them, and we make it our intention with love, humility, acceptance, and authenticity. I've had many relationships in my life that have either failed or have been strained. My dad and I had a "see-saw" relationship, as I'm sure many of you have had with your parents, and there were times when I blamed him, judged him, didn't understand him. I was too young or too immature, or my consciousness couldn't really see what he was trying to prepare me for or protect me from. The pains of the future he saw for me were based on his consciousness at the time.

But I feel really blessed, whole, and complete that we were able to come together and find that love and mutual respect to honour each other in our later years. I'm so grateful that we found peace before the last years of his life. Like that, I've had so many other relationships where there was a strain, and for those that really mattered to me, I made the conscious choice to reach out and work at them - to have conversations that helped bring healing in those relationships. I realised the distinction between acceptance and forgiveness. With forgiveness, there is the presupposition that someone was "wrong," and hence the relationship needed forgiving, but when I was able to let go of either of us being right or wrong, then acceptance was all that was required.

What comes to mind is this beautiful art form from Japan, called Kintsugi (also known as Kintsukuroi). The method of restoring breakage with gold translates as "golden joinery," an outgrowth of Wabi-Sabi's Japanese philosophy, which honours the beauty of imperfections. When a ceramic or porcelain vase or bowl breaks, they glue the pieces back together using liquid gold instead of throwing it away, making it even more valuable, even more precious than it was before it was broken. Similarly, when you start to mend and heal your relationships with the gold of love, they become more valuable.

Let's do a quick exercise together using the wisdom of the body. Pick one area from your wheel of life that you'd like to focus on for now. Think about your desire to have it, then stand up and use your dominant arm and hand to answer this question. Start with both hands pointing down at the floor; this is zero per cent. Now, if you were to raise that arm and point your fingers all the way up to the ceiling, that is one hundred per cent. How much do you desire this something that you put in your wheel of life? Now, allow your hand to answer.

Let me share my example of wanting to lose weight. My hand went all the way up, pointing at the ceiling, which shows that I really want it. I hope you did the same thing with your goal. Just see where your hand went up to. For example, how much do you want to start this new business that you've been thinking about? How much do you want to mend this particular relationship?

Now relax both arms and shake them out. I'm going to ask you a second question. How much energy and action have you been putting into making this a reality? With my example of how much effort I had been putting into losing weight and being slimmer, I let my hand answer, and it went up to about 120 degrees. In approximate percentage, I would say it went up to about eighty per cent. It didn't go all the way up to point at the ceiling, which would have been one hundred per cent.

Where did your hand go? Now notice the gap. Very often, we think we want something fully. However, we're not putting all of us into it. Coming back to my example, if I were to be truly honest, when I did this, I only went up to eighty per cent, not to one hundred per cent, and that's why I hadn't been able to shed the few extra kilos yet. So, what was in that gap? I didn't exercise every single day. I exercised eighty per cent of the week, true. I didn't watch my food all the time. In that twenty per cent delta, I could already identify the things that I could still do to really give this goal my one hundred per cent were. My arm answered the question for me accurately. Perhaps at this point in your life, another goal is taking priority, and that is fine, as long as you are aware. Becoming consciously aware of your shift in priorities will help take away any negative emotion of frustration you have towards this particular goal.

With your top priority goals, check in with yourself — how much energy, resources, action, and commitment are you putting into your goals, and then check the gap. Next, note for yourself what is still missing. What else can you do? What more energy can you give to it? Even if you are unsure what the next step could be, take a small action that seems most accessible. It could be to reach out or reconnect with someone; it could be to research something, do something, just about anything. What little action can you start to put in? What seeds can you use to plant that would raise you to one hundred per cent? How many resources in the form of time, money, and energy could you really "spend" on your relationships if you were truly committed to nurturing them?

When it comes to taking action, we need our bodies. We need our voice to speak, our fingers to type those emails and messages, our legs to take us around. Our bodies help to facilitate the inspired action that will take us closer to living the life we want. The way we hold and move our bodies can inform and affect our emotional states.

In the workbook on the resource page (https://maltibhojwani.com/myl.html), practice four dispositions of powerful presence to help you gain access to different ways of holding and moving your body to help you shift your mood and mindset. I attribute this field of knowledge to Carl Jung, Mark Walsh, and the Newfield coach training, where I learned it over twenty years ago.

CHAPTER 8:
STAYING THE COURSE —
"BOUNCE-BACK-ABILITY"

We've come to the final chapter of mastering your life. The word "final" sounds like the end; however, it's only the beginning.

"Some people are so afraid to die that they never begin to live."
- Henry Van Dyke

The last exercise we're going to do together is writing your eulogy.

A eulogy is a speech or piece of writing praising someone or something highly, especially a tribute to someone who has just died. We hide from death, but it is guaranteed; you're not getting out of here alive. Writing your own eulogy will inspire you to reflect on your mortality and the impermanence of your body and ego even though your soul is timeless. It will also create a more profound sense of urgency to choose what you want to do with the rest of your life.

So pause now, take a few moments, find a piece of paper, and imagine that someone you love is on stage dedicating a speech to your life. If you find a eulogy too morbid, then write it as if it was your birthday party.

Start by writing your name, then write the overarching state-ment you want to be remembered for. For example, *"Malti Bhojwani was a woman who never gave up. She went against conditioned beliefs and had the courage to..."*

What do you want people to be saying about you long after you're gone? What adjectives do you want them to use to describe you? What do they say you lived for? What values did you live so loudly that it was seen in everything that you did?

Writing your own eulogy is one of the most powerful stories you can ever write or rewrite. Imagine what your closest friend, one of your mentees, perhaps a grandchild would say about you? What would you like them to say? If you keep going on the way you are now? Changing nothing? What would they say? Would they be able to see your purpose through your life actions? What sort of father, grandfather, son, partner would you like to be remembered as? What type of mother, grandmother, daughter, sister, colleague, team mem-ber, and leader would you like to be remembered as? What do you want your priorities to say about you?

"You are the Creator of Your Life."

What did you do with your time? As you know, what we do with our time on this planet shows what our priorities are. What roles did you play? What legacy did you leave? What compliments would you like to have received throughout your life? What accomplish-ments would you like to be remembered for? What do your family members say about you? What do your friends say about you? What was the first impression or the last impression you left on the people around you?

If this was a three to five-minute speech, what would be the tone of the speech? Is it funny? Is it joyful? Is it sombre? This is your opportunity to decide today and create today what the rest of your life will look like because once you've written your own eulogy, subconsciously and consciously, you will be living up to it.

If you've done that already, then after a few days, check-in with yourself using the kinesiology technique that I shared with you earlier. Use your dominant hand, raise it up to ninety degrees, pointing at a wall in front of you, and then ask yourself, how fully am I already living my values? My purpose? How close am I to living this vision of myself that I have written about in this eulogy? Then allow your hand to answer. Does it go all the way up? Does it stay at fifty per cent? Does it go down? And then you will know for yourself. This is not to judge yourself, not to feel guilty, not to blame yourself. It's only about looking in the mirror, accepting with compassion for yourself, and realising that you are creating the rest of your life today as the creator of your life who chooses to live and enjoy this life. Instead of just trying to run away from death or just trying to survive, you can live up to your eulogy and more. If you choose to enjoy this life, then how will you live the rest of your days?

I would love to know that I died trying at anything that I ever wanted to create or do in my life, that at least at the end, I'd be able to say that I died trying. I kept trying. Because if we keep going, and we don't stop, then we never ever fail, do we? If we are able to keep doing it over and over, finding the grit and resilience, finding the energy to keep getting up each time we fall, then we never really lose, do we?

I have seen friends, colleagues, mentors, and teachers who are much older than I am who are still trying, still reinventing themselves, innovating, learning, and still going out there and trying new things day by day, and they inspire me.

Just like trees, we either grow or we die. If we don't have a mindset of growth, a mindset to learn, evolve, let go of the old, and keep trying, we will become complacent, bored, miserable, and die.

There are two kinds of motivation — "away from" and "towards." Away from motivation is trying to get away from what we don't want. For example, "I don't want to be penniless," "I don't want to be alone," "I don't want to be overweight," "I don't want to be a terrible leader," or "I don't want to be a failure in my life." This is one kind of motivation. It may work but only to a certain extent. Imagine having a tiger chasing you your whole life, and you just have to keep running away from it. It gets exhausting.

However, when we connect with our purpose, we have "toward motivation" — living towards what we do want. This is so much more attractive and acts like a magnet, drawing us towards life mastery. Moving towards life, living, and enjoying life with joy is so much more beautiful than running away from what could kill us. It ensures that each morning, we will wake up excited, happy, and enthused.

And I mean more than just the widely accepted definition of the word "enthused." In Greek, the word is "enthousiasmos," which means "divine inspiration; to be inspired or possessed by a god; to be rapt; to be in ecstasy." And by breaking down the word into its root parts, we understand why: en or "in" + theos or "god" = in God. So let us all live our lives "enthused."

Essentially, it boils down to embracing and accepting death in order to truly start living, enjoying. Fears are merely a doubt that we may not be able to do, be, or have what we think we need to survive this life. But when we embrace death, we don't need anything more than what we already have. When we have no needs, then we have no fears. We can truly savour and relish each sublime day and enjoy this gift of life. Anything more is just "nice to have" accessories. Because what we have right now is more than enough to truly enjoy our lives.

If death is inevitable, then I want to die with dignity. Dying with dignity for me is to have lived a life where I continued to endeavour to pursue happiness. We spend our lives trying to prevent death by eating, loving, fighting, praying, but what if death is a continuum and that life is tob e simply enjoyed while preparing us for what comes after?

"Happiness is the meaning and the purpose of life,
the whole aim and end of human existence."
- Aristotle

"Resilience" is the emotional and mental ability to keep bouncing back every time we encounter a challenge. If we can look at each challenge as an opportunity and find the learnings, we keep bouncing back. Now, how do we build that resilience in our minds? It's through having a positive attitude and reframing our thoughts. Resilience is built over time when we are not stressed. Think of it as charging your batteries and strengthening the trampoline before you need it so that when you do need it, you are able to take the proverbial hits.

"You can have many excuses and reasons to quit, or you can have results. Which would you prefer? One thousand reasons as to why you quit or one thousand attempts = one thousand different results to learn from?"- MB

Building the muscle of resilience cultivates the inner knowing that every attempt is getting us closer to where we say we want to go, not getting demotivated. Of course, we experience grief, sadness, and disappointment when things don't work out the way we'd love them to. This is when we can pause, feel the pain, rest, and embrace what we are feeling fully so that we can let it go. And remembering that "many roads lead to Rome," and even if we didn't "get" what we thought we "should have," we have faith that something better is in store for us.

Rest helps to build resilience. When we exercise, we are advised to rest the muscles because we want to allow them to heal and strengthen. Similarly, mentally and emotionally, we need rest and sleep. There's wisdom in the adage "Sleep on it." Sometimes, the best thing to do is close your eyes and take a nap or meditate when you're unsure what to do next. Even Einstein made some of his most innovative discoveries while he was "doing nothing". Don't feel guilty about rest time or downtime; look at it as plugging yourself into your charger to get recharged so that you have more energy. You will emerge more intuitive and creative to get up and take action again.

Take time to grieve. Take time to be disappointed. It's okay. We can't prevent our emotions, and we shouldn't bury them. We feel what we feel, and in fact, the most powerful healing we can do for ourselves is to allow ourselves to really feel them, not suppress, deflect, or resist them. We can't tell ourselves that it's wrong to feel sad. As we first embrace then let go of our painful, fearful emotions, we are becoming more and more the creator of our destinies, the master of our lives.

My dear friend lost both her teenage daughter and her husband within six years of each other. Now, many people would have curled up in misery, but she knew that life was still a gift, and she only had two choices: to be miserable or to be grateful for her days with them and thankful for each day she now had. She chose to live in gratitude, rejoicing in what she could still have and do. And she took action — from baking and decorating beautiful cakes to learning to dance. It's inspiring to behold her awesomeness and resilience. So, if she is any example for you, resilience and the ability to bounce back is crucial when you embark on making radical changes in your life.

"Resistance is proportionate to the size and speed of the change, not to whether the change is a favourable or unfavourable one."
- George Leonard, Mastery

In biology, this tendency to want to return to stability and find equilibrium is called homeostasis. It is imperative in our bodies because this is what regulates our blood pressure, making our hearts beat faster when it dips, ensuring our temperature stays within the healthy range, etc. You can liken it to a thermostat in a reverse-cycle airconditioner: when we set it to a certain temperature, it will automatically regulate to maintain it.

Similarly, in our day-to-day lifestyles, we settle into our own equilibrium. When we embark on creating changes in our lifestyle and belief systems, the natural tendency of a human being is to regain that balance.

Let me share a simplified ancient analogy used to explain this, described by Plato in The Allegory of the Cave (514a–520a).

Once upon a time, a few men were tied to a stone in a cave for so long that they had forgotten what the world looked like outside of the dark cave. Their world view was limited to the darkness and confines of the cave. One day, one of the men found the courage to free himself. However, once outside, because of the overwhelming stimuli from the twinkling of the stars at night to the brightness of the sun, his eyes could not stay open. It was too blinding compared to what his eyes were accustomed to from his years in the cave. In the story, he hurried back into the cave to find his old "normal again" as it felt safer and more familiar than in the light. He told his cave-mates what he had seen, urging them to come out and have a look too, but instead of encouragement, he was mocked and ridiculed because none of them believed him.

What if, however, he had improvised, worn a blindfold to help him adjust and moderate the amount of light reaching his eyes, and taken baby steps to appreciate and absorb the "new world"? What if he had inspired his cave-mates slowly rather than frantically trying to force them out of the cave too?

Similarly, when we start to step outside our limiting beliefs, our old normal, we challenge not only ourselves but the people around us who have been so comfortable having us where they could understand and relate to us without having to change themselves.

Research in family constellation has shown that a family seeks to maintain its customary organisation and functioning over time, often destroying itself and resisting any change in an effort to keep this sense of balance or homeostasis. In Latin, homeostasis means "same status."

When we choose to accelerate our personal growth and evolution, the dynamics in our relationships will inevitably change, causing discomfort for the people around us who are not ready to awaken themselves.

I have been blessed with a husband, mother, daughter, brothers, friends, and colleagues who not only accept me the way I am but who have been a strong force in beholding me whilst I have grown. My father supported my choices to break free from societal norms. My husband shared his abundance mindset with me, which at one time even earned me four times more the salary I was willing to settle for! Unfortunately, this may not be the case for all of us with our loved ones. You will naturally find over time that the people who stay in your life are replenishing and nourishing your energy whilst the ones who have slipped away from you were draining your energy.

Coming back to the cave analogy, what you can do to coax the people who matter most in your life out of their metaphorical cave is to enjoy your life. Light some candles, play some music, diffuse some aromatic uplifting oils outside figuratively or literally, and hope that your beloved cave dwellers will be intrigued enough to join you and step out slowly to see, taste, smell, and hear for themselves. Be mindful however of becoming "that person" — the "spiritually egotistical" or the "guru" who tries to force their own insights down the throats of others. Spiritual arrogance is an oxymoron, so pause to assess why you are about to say what you want to. Is it to show yourself as superior and others as inferior, or is it truly to serve? Nothing can repel people from finding love, joy, and the ultimate truth when they are not yet ready than someone pushing their personal epiphanies onto them.

Knowledge is power, and what I've endeavoured to do in this book is to share with you every single gem of wisdom that I've learned through my life experiences and the work and study that I have committed my life to. With this knowledge comes the opportunity to practice because knowledge without practice is useless. I recently started to learn how to play the piano, and more plainly than ever, I am realising how my weekly lessons are only the "knowledge." However, the actual learning embeds itself when I practice the most mundane and straightforward routines daily with diligence and allow the lessons to sink in when I sleep and meditate. I trust that they will eventually culminate in me being able to play the songs I love. We can read stacks of books, go to tons of workshops, do multiple programs, but if we don't put the knowledge into practice, nothing can really come out of it.

"Knowledge is POWER, but practice is MASTERY."
- MB

Remember, the OAR model we shared at the start of this book — the observer does the action; the actions create the results. You have shifted the observer that you are, and now, with this wisdom, it's time for you to put it all into practice. Keep getting up every time you fall, scratch it off, and move on over and over, as Puff Johnson says in her song. Don't stop, and you will never fail. Practice making choices saying "yes" and "no" based on your gut, knowing when to stop something. Letting go of the fear of missing out is liberating.

Practice centring a few times a day. Do your two-word purpose exercise and live in integrity with what fulfils you. If you haven't yet done it, do it with friends and family. It is so wonderful to share these happy memories with each other. Do it with your team; it has been proven to bring teams together. Create your vision board, go through your wheel of life, be honest with yourself, go back to check your results from the beginning of this book, and look at how you would rank your wheel of life now in all the different areas of your life through your new lens.

Go to Barrett's link and check your top ten values. Again, do it with your partner, your friends, your team, or your kids. Relationships become so much easier when we understand each other's values. Make sure you have a regular meditation practice apart from the guided meditations that I've recommended and do the silent practice as well. Join me in my live sessions, and I will teach it to you. In the meantime, download an app and meditate. Practice pausing and practise responding rather than reacting to life's circumstances.

Practice making choices in the moment the next time you're triggered, and you're about to say something that you might later regret. Ask yourself, for what sake am I about to say what I'm about to say? Is it to be right? To have the last word, or is it really going to show love and kindness? Is it truly me living from my purpose and my values? Well, pause before you say it because you can either be right or be happy in your relationships. You can't be both all of the time. Being self-righteous and "right about our opinions" comes from lower frequency emotions, like the fear of being seen as wrong, the arrogance about being right, and the pay-offs from feeling haughty about being "such a smart and good person" (in inverted commas).

"Sometimes the most important thing in a whole day is the rest we take between two deep breaths." - Etty Hillesum

Finally, allow yourself to rest and to sleep. Take care of yourself. Self-care and self-love are essential for your worthiness and your self-esteem. Any happy thought you can conjure, a daydream or memory that makes your lips curl ever so slightly in a smile, any giggle or chuckle you can evoke through a funny thought or a joke will lift your mood. Even watching a scene from a comedy show (my current go-to are re-runs of "Friends"), anything that makes you connect to love, joy, gratitude and humour will lift your frequency instantly. Indulge guiltlessly. It is good for you!

"Be kind whenever possible. It's always possible."
- Dalai Lama

EPILOGUE:
DYING WITH DIGNITY

The paradox of mastering your life lies in the balance between staying in the flow of life whilst not gripping onto it. What does it mean to be enlightened, to be awakened? It's that moment when we wake up when we see the light and it shines through the beliefs and paradigm that kept us separate from oneness with Source, when we realise that we indeed are spiritual beings having a human experience, one that we chose to experience.

The paradox is that we spend half our lives fighting to earn and deserve the life that we want when, in fact, we were already born worthy. We don't have to do anything. We don't have to prove anything. We don't have to earn anything. We don't even have real needs. We are worthy from the womb to the tomb. From the moment of our very conception, we were worthy of the nutrients and the nourishment that came to us as a birthright through our mothers because we were already worthy. We received everything we needed, unconditionally supported by nature. It's a paradox because we then grow up, and we forget that we are indeed worthy.

Awakening is like dreaming, yet knowing that you are the dreamer, enjoying the dream, and at the same time not forcing ourselves to wake up. For some of us, it may feel like a knowing; for some of us, it's a spark. And for some of us, it's a burst of laughter we have the moment we realise that we're already all we sought to become.

Once we have shifted that very root perspective of life, we will never be able to go back and pretend that we don't know what we know. It's like the caterpillar that becomes a butterfly and never realised that he was already a butterfly inside. This is when life is enjoyed rather than merely being endured.

"It's the soul afraid of dying, that never learns to live"
– Bette Midler – The Rose.

You may think it's easy for me to say all these things that seem cliché because my life is working for me now. But it's the other way around. It's only when I saw who I really am — a spirit being human in the embodiment of Malti Bhojwani — stepped into my worthiness and started believing that joy is indeed my birthright that I began to see beauty manifest in my life. When we live from this truth, then the universe gives us little gifts, little signs along the way, that help us reinforce and strengthen our knowing that we are indeed creating our best lives. I already have all that I've ever wanted beyond my imagination.

My father's passing to the light happened just before COVID-19 hit, and I was able to witness a great man die with dignity. He never gave up in life, always having the willingness to learn new things, even to his very last days, and in the end, he accepted death with elegance and grace, just saying goodbye, very matter-of-factly to all of us. And I let go with gratitude his beliefs around survival, and welcomed strongly his "yes-attitude", courage, resilience, energy for life and passion.

I'm no longer just living to get away from death to survive this life, but I am really living to enjoy this life. The cherry blossom, Sakura, represents both the fragility and the beauty of life. It's a reminder that life is breathtakingly beautiful but that it is also short. See today as the start of Spring in your life, like the cherry blossom when they are in full bloom; your future is bursting with possibilities.

Step off the brakes of fear, feel the wind on your face and smile in gratitude as life loves you back. I feel privileged to have partnered with you so far. My hope for you is that you too have come to that realisation for yourself and that you go on and start celebrating your already amazing life, knowing that you, the observer, have always been the observed, the see-er and the seen, the soul and the self — you have always been divine. Celebration is the ultimate form of gratitude, the quintessential form of enjoyment. So, I'm going to celebrate my charmed life, and I hope the same for you.

"And those who were seen dancing were thought to be insane by those who could not hear the music."
- Friedrich Nietzsche

THE END

Look out for Malti's live meditation sessions
and her latest work on
www.maltibhojwani.com.

Subscribe to her YouTube channel maltibhojwani to stay
connected and informed.

Find the workbook and resources
mentioned in this book on
bit.ly/masteringyourlife or maltibhojwani.com/myl.html